GIVE ME WISDOM

*Practical Principles for
Living a God-Guided Life*

PAMELA R. MALONE

GIVE ME WISDOM

Practical Principles for Living a God-Guided Life

Copyright © 2025 by Pamela R. Malone

All rights reserved. No part of this book may be reproduced or transmitted in any form or by any means without written permission from the author.

Build A Brother
PUBLISHING

ACKNOWLEDGMENTS

I want to give thanks to God, my creator, to whom I am nothing without His constant hand on my life. Thank you for speaking to me when I was at a loss for what to write, I stayed steadfast, and You spoke to me. To my husband, my greatest encourager who has always seen what I at times failed to see in myself, an abundance of potential. Thank you for reminding me that potential is not a compliment; it only speaks to what you have the ability to do but didn't, so do not sit on what God gifted you with. I have done things I never thought I could do because you pushed me out of my comfort zone.

To my children, Ashley, Andrea, Carlos Jr., Raye, and my bonus son, Derby, you all are the greatest gifts God has given to me. I am proud to be your mother, and I pray that this book will inspire you in your walk with God. Lastly, to my parents, Mom, you are one of the strongest women I know. You made sure my siblings and I were introduced to Christ at an early age. Thank you for prioritizing what was important and for the countless sacrifices you made raising my siblings and me after Dad passed when we were still so young.

Mom, you may not be able to read this novel due to a condition beyond your control. I hope to at least capture a picture of you holding it in your hands. Dad, you have been gone for over 56 years, I'd like to think you are looking down on me smiling, saying, "That's my girl."

CONTENTS

Introduction	1
Chapter One: What Is Wisdom	9
Chapter Two: How To Obtain Wisdom	17
Chapter Three: The Character of Wisdom	29
Chapter Four: Listen Up	41
Chapter Five: The Protection of Wisdom	51
Chapter Six: The Danger in Ignoring Wisdom's Voice	69
Chapter Seven: Living Your Blessed Life	81
Chapter Eight: The Courage & Faithfulness of Wisdom	89
Closing Thoughts	107
About The Author	109

Proverbs 9:10-12 (NLT2)

[10] Fear of the LORD is the foundation of wisdom. Knowledge of the Holy One results in good judgment.

[11] Wisdom will multiply your days and add years to your life.

[12] If you become wise, you will be the one to benefit. If you scorn wisdom, you will be the one to suffer.

Proverbs 2:1-6 (NLT2)

[1] My child, listen to what I say, and treasure my commands.

[2] Tune your ears to wisdom, and concentrate on understanding.

[3] Cry out for insight, and ask for understanding.

[4] Search for them as you would for silver; seek them like hidden treasures.

[5] Then you will understand what it means to fear the LORD, and you will gain knowledge of God.

[6] For the LORD grants wisdom! From his mouth come knowledge and understanding.

1 Kings 3:7-10 (NLT2)

[7] "Now, O LORD my God, you have made me king instead of my father, David, but I am like a little child who doesn't know his way around.

[8] And here I am in the midst of your own chosen people, a nation so great and numerous they cannot be counted!

[9] Give me an understanding heart so that I can govern your people well and know the difference between right and wrong. For who by himself is able to govern this great people of yours?"

[10] The Lord was pleased that Solomon had asked for wisdom.

Proverbs 16:16 (AMP)

[16] How much better it is to get skillful and godly Wisdom than gold! And to get understanding is to be chosen rather than silver.

Job 12:13 (NLT2)

[13] "But true wisdom and power are found in God; counsel and understanding are his.

Introduction

1 Kings 3:7-13 (NLT2)
⁷ "Now, O LORD my God, you have made me king instead of my father, David, but I am like a little child who doesn't know his way around.

⁸ And here I am in the midst of your own chosen people, a nation so great and numerous they cannot be counted!

⁹ Give me an understanding heart so that I can govern your people well and know the difference between right and wrong. For who by himself is able to govern this great people of yours?"

¹⁰ The Lord was pleased that Solomon had asked for wisdom.

¹¹ So God replied, "Because you have asked for wisdom in governing my people with justice and have not asked for a long life or wealth or the death of your enemies—

¹² I will give you what you asked for! I will give you a wise and understanding heart such as no one else has had or ever will have!

¹³ And I will also give you what you did not ask for—riches and fame! No other king in all the world will be compared to you for the rest of your life!

An extraordinary request from one of God's servants who knew his limitations. When you think you are wiser than you really are, you will exclude the One from your life who really is. Out of everything Solomon could have requested of God, he sought not from God the thing that would give him the most pleasure, but he chose instead the thing that would please God the most; wisdom to lead God's people. How rewarding the life of the believer would be if they understood what Solomon realized in that moment; God I cannot do this thing called life without your guidance, I need your insight if I am going to be good at my assignment. If you and I are going to be successful in life, we too will need wisdom in order to do it. We need wisdom to know the difference between making good decisions from wrong decisions; knowing God's perspective on a situation verses our own. Embracing wisdom empowers us to make choices, aligning with God's vision. Surrendering to His guidance, unlocks a life of purpose fueled by His wisdom and love. Let's be honest; some of the chaos we experience in life is not always brought on by the enemy but by our own decision making and our lack of knowledge of how we are to live.

Hosea 4:6 (KJV)

⁶ My people are destroyed for lack of knowledge: because thou hast rejected knowledge. The people had rejected God the one who is all knowing.

When you reject God, life has nowhere to go but in a downward spiral. Life begins with God. Who better to direct your life than the one who gave you the gift of life. You would not go to a plumber to tell you how your car works. That would not make sense, you would go to the manufacturer of the vehicle. The creator of your life is the only person who should be instructing you on your life and how it is to be lived. Wisdom is one of the most valuable possessions the believer can attain. Proverbs says this: *¹⁶ How much better it is to get skillful and godly Wisdom than gold! And to get understanding is to be chosen rather than silver.* ***Proverbs 16:16 (AMP)*** Nothing in life is better than Wisdom, not even money. Listen to the words of, **Ecclesiastes 7:11-12 (AMP)** ¹¹ Wisdom is as good as an inheritance, yes, more excellent it is for those [the living] who see the sun.

[12] For wisdom is a defense even as money is a defense, but the excellency of knowledge is that wisdom shields *and* preserves the life of him who has it. Wisdom is more valuable than the money you have. We've all heard stories of people who were once wealthy and ended up totally broke not long after. What good is wealth if you do not have the wisdom on how to maintain it? Wisdom is a defense that protects you and me daily when we yield to wisdom's leading. Both wisdom and money benefit us as we go through life, however, wisdom can save your life in ways your money cannot. By this I mean, money can provide solutions to certain life-threatening things after the fact, however; wisdom offers the ability to gain insight before making a life altering decision in order to prevent a disastrous outcome. Here is what you need to know, wisdom is not head knowledge but God knowledge! God knowledge on a matter trumps knowledge from any other source, period!

Money is a wonderful thing to have but which would you rather have? For me it is the thing that can save my life. There is no better way to experience life than to understand how life is meant to be lived. We all have been given life; one I'd like to believe we each want to make the best of. Life at times can be challenging, other times it can be easy. Life at times is similar to traveling down a road. There are smooth roads that are easy to drive on and then there are bumpy roads, some that include large potholes which we'd all rather avoid. Let's be real, if you are like me, you like to travel the path of least resistance. Look at it this way, we all want to avoid unnecessary hazards when driving. There are straight roads and there are winding roads that can cause significant danger if you are not focused as you should be. I'll never forget the time I was in the vehicle with my daughter who was driving at the time. It was dark and we were traveling down a road neither of us were familiar with. She came upon a curve she had not anticipated, driving at a speed that was not appropriate when approaching a curve. Needless to say, she scared the living daylights out of the two of us. We are grateful to have remained on the road and not over the cliff as I was screaming at the top of my lungs, CURVE! This is as clean as I can explain my reaction.

Life sometimes throws us unexpected curves, which come with twists and turns, unexpected conflicts, tests, and decisions. The decision to do what's right or to do what's wrong; to live godly or ungodly, to be harmful or to be helpful, to be obedient or disobedient; to be honest or dishonest; the list goes on. How we choose to live life; and what we get out of life, whether good or bad, depends upon the things we allow to influence our lives, but more importantly, who we allow to influence and control our lives. If you are honest with yourself, you can admit, no one wants to, or even likes the thought of surrendering control of one's life to someone else. No one wants to be constantly told what to do, what not to do, what to say, what not to say, when to speak and when to keep quiet; after all we are not puppets, moving by the strings of someone else's hands.

We all like having our way and having our say; even at times when we are the only ones in agreement with ourselves. If we are brutally honest with ourselves, there are times our judgments, actions and beliefs aren't always what's right, what's needed or what's best at times. We all need a voice of reason to help prevent us from acting foolishly, thinking foolishly and speaking foolishly. How many times have you thought or said if only I had someone in my life to assist me from making senseless mistakes, I could have saved myself a lot of heartache, and trouble; I could have saved myself a lot of wasted days, weeks, months, even years of failed attempts at living a victorious life; instead of one that consist of countless defeats. Well, you are not alone, have been there, done that, and I can say it was not a joyful time in my life either.

There comes a time when you have to tell yourself my way is not working; there has to be a better way of doing things than the way I've been doing them. There has to be a successful way of living, where I'm winning more than losing. I'm here to let you in on a little secret, you do have help. Every born-again believer has always had readily available help. From the very moment you accepted Jesus as Savior and acknowledged God as Father; from the moment we choose to let God guide our lives; we have had access to an incredible Spiritual Intelligence to assist us in navigating life. (More on this intelligence later in the book).Our heavenly Father knew you and I would not be able to conquer life's challenges on our own. Being cognizant of our limitation God provides wisdom as a loving, caring parent would. Wisdom is always imparting guidance and direction; but are His children receptive to wisdom's counsel? More on this in chapter entitled "Listen Up."

Proverbs 4:7-8 (NLT2)
⁷ Getting wisdom is the wisest thing you can do! And whatever else you do, develop good judgment.
⁸ If you prize wisdom, she will make you great. Embrace her, and she will honor you.

Proverbs 8:1-3 (NLT2)
¹ Listen as Wisdom calls out! Hear as understanding raises her voice!
² On the hilltop along the road, she takes her stand at the crossroads.
³ By the gates at the entrance to the town, on the road leading in, she cries aloud,

Here in Proverbs the instructor uses a feminine verb to describe wisdom, why men should listen to women more often. I'm just kidding, we do not possess all the answers, even though at times we feel as though we do. Wisdom here is a concept devoid of biological gender. As stated in John 4:24. " God is Spirit." He is not feminine in any shape form or fashion, so there is no confusion here. My objective is to inspire and remind you to pursue the insight and understanding that is readily available and accessible to every child of God, through wisdoms guidance. Please keep this in mind when verses from Proverbs are discussed later on in the reading of the book. Identification break over, back to our topic of discussion.

I for one am happy that God thought of everything concerning my needs. On my best days, the days I think I have it altogether; the days I've done my research on a matter; weighed all my options; and planned for any potential hiccups, I'm subject to do something stupid, if I rely totally on my intellect alone. There are times God's creation can think we are smarter than we really are, and that can get us into trouble. Life comes with enough trouble of its own, we don't need any additional trouble by thinking we are smarter than we really are. There is only one person when it comes to decision making, who has a level of intelligence which surpasses that of all mankind; one single person who counsels only with Himself; one person, who is all knowing and all wise; that is God Himself. Here is how I Corinthians 1:25 describes the wisdom of God to that of man.

I Corinthians 1:25 (KJV)
"The foolishness of God is wiser than men." With all man's planning he is no more than a mere fool when he lives his life without the aid and counsel of God.

At man's smartest, he is still dumber than God! There is no given day where man's intellect can stand up to God's wisdom. God can ask man a simple question and have man telling on himself without him even realizing it. When Adam and Eve were hiding from God in the Garden of Eden after they had sinned, God asked Adam, "where art thou?" Without ever mentioning to God, he had eaten from the forbidden tree, Adam had told on himself. All Adam said was "I was naked; so, I hid." Listen to what God says to Adam.

Genesis 3:11 (KJV).
[11] "Who told thee that thou wast naked? Hast, thou eaten of the tree, whereof I commanded thee that thou shouldest not eat?

In that moment when Adam said I was naked, so I hid, God knew Adam had disobeyed Him, that's how smart God is. When God questions his children, it's not because He's seeking an answer to the unknown, He already knows the answer. It's not revelation God is seeking, it's the confession He's seeking from you and I in order to make things right with Him again. That's the wisdom of an all-knowing God; He can do something as simple as ask you and I a question and we end up telling on ourselves without realizing it; subsequently squandering the blessings God intended for His children to have. Let's face it, just like Adam, every part of God's creation is inherently subject to making mistakes. These errors can sometimes come at a great cost, making recovery seemingly impossible, but for the grace of God. The price paid for these mistakes should serve as a lasting reminder of the limitations and imperfections you and I have.

As His children, we do not have to live in ignorance, making costly mistakes one after the other. There are traps we can avoid when we rely on what I like to refer to as our **Spiritual Intelligence, named Wisdom**, and it is ours for the asking, according to James.

James 1:5
"If any of you lack wisdom, let him ask of God, that giveth to all men liberally, and upbraideth not; and it shall be given him"

I will discuss James 1:5 in more detail in a later chapter but let me say this; you and I have this power source to help us navigate our way through life's ups and downs, that we don't rely on as often as I think we should and all we have to do is ask our Heavenly Father to supply us with it. No matter our plans, the choices we make, or the situations we face in life, applying God's wisdom is crucial to the outcome of things. When we operate in His wisdom, the end results will always be what's best for the situation.

Journey with me as we take an in-depth look concerning wisdom and the numerous ways it is beneficial in the believer's life. Will this book share with you in total everything there is to know about wisdom? No, but my desire is to expand your view of the vital role wisdom plays in your life and urge you to cherish it, cling to it as though your life depends on it, because it truly does. It truly is essential to your existence!

Chapter One

What Is Wisdom

Let me be clear, there are two kinds of wisdom: worldly wisdom and Godly wisdom. There is a vast difference between the two.

Worldly Wisdom: *self-confidence and self-knowledge and understanding which comes through human sources.*

Don't get me wrong, not all human wisdom is bad, I have benefitted from the wisdom of others. I am a better person today because of the words of wisdom and instruction I have received from my parents, teachers, friends and spiritual leaders. I'm not saying abandon instruction and insight from people who have been an immense help in your life. The point I'm making is, it's not wise to solely rely on human wisdom alone. While human teachings provide a valuable foundation, Spiritual wisdom extends beyond what is taught through the scale of humanity. Humanity at times is flawed in its ideology. Humanity also has its limitations when it comes to knowledge. Humanity has the tendency to think it is wiser than it really is. There will be times in your life that it's not man's insight on a matter that you need but rather God's. Truthfully speaking, if we sought God more, we wouldn't need human guidance as much. I get it, we all need somebody, but we should never rely on humanity more than God, God never intended for us to live this way. *Here is my simple definition of Godly wisdom.*

Godly Wisdom: *an enlightenment or insight of knowledge and understanding that cannot be attained through human source; it is a Spiritual level of dimension that allows the believer to have awareness from God's perspective.*

This is why I refer to wisdom as the believer's source of Spiritual Intelligence. In the United States we have what is called Intelligence. Intelligence is information gathered within or outside the United States that involves threats to our nation; its people, property; interests; development, proliferation, or use of weapons of mass destruction; and any other matter bearing on the U.S. national or homeland security. Intelligence can provide insights not available elsewhere that warn of potential threats and opportunities, assess probable outcomes of proposed policy options, provide leadership profiles on foreign officials, and inform official travelers of counterintelligence and security threats. (Director of National intelligence) From this definition of intelligence, we see the key objective of intelligence is to gather information that involves threats of any kind to the nation, its people, property, or interests in order to keep the country and its citizens protected. This is one of the main purposes of wisdom; to help God's children recognize and avoid all threats that are detrimental to their Christian walk. The importance of wisdom in the believer's life should not be downplayed. Proverbs state this:

Proverbs 4:6-7:
Don't turn your back on wisdom, for she will protect you, love her and she will guard you.

Wisdom safeguards you and I when we prioritize her in our lives. Wisdom forewarns you and I of dangers that we at times are unaware of. I don't know about you, but I for one like the idea of knowing about potential threats in advance. The purpose of advance notice is to prepare you ahead of time, so you are not caught off guard, or taken out by the threat. I, along with millions of other US citizens, wished forty-five would have used wisdom in the handling of Covid 19. He ignored the knowledge of people who had more insight on the disease and matter than he did. He had been forewarned of the devastation that would occur to the millions of US citizens if He did not act quickly and responsibly. Instead, he downplayed the severity of the situation, and we all ended up in a pandemic that cost millions of people their lives. We had a man leading the country who listened to himself 99% of the time and 1% of the time to others; that's a recipe for disaster. There were people in place to help him to not only understand the magnitude of the situation but were qualified to oversee the situation. He, however, chose instead to operate according to his own wisdom, ignoring the wisdom of trained, qualified personnel who have knowledge and understanding that superseded that of his own.

When you do not have a clear understanding of the importance of a thing, the need for it, and how it works, you can rob yourself of the full benefits that come with it and how it can best serve you. I remember when I first began using this Bible program, I have called Wordsearch." I had been using this program for a long time before I realized that I had not tapped into everything the bible program offered. I loved using it because of the multiple resources it contained, such as various Bible translations,

Strong's Concordances and dictionaries amongst many other resources. I no longer had to have multiple books spread out on the table as I studied. I'm the type of teacher who likes putting complete scripture reference in my document. As per usual I would look up the scripture and type the scripture into my document; until one day I decided to view the video tutorials that came with the program. Unbeknownst to me, I had this powerful tool called "ZipScript" at my disposal to make documenting the scripture(s) effortless. It was always available, but I had to seek it out. It wasn't hidden in a secret location where I did not have access, it was always within reach.

Zip-Script enabled me to type the chapter plus the range of verses, and it would insert the scriptures right into my document for me, easy breezy." I spent a lot of wasted time typing what I did not need to when I had in my possession a powerful source to help me do what I needed to do with ease. If I wanted the scripture in several translations, it would copy every translation I selected over into my document all at once. This is what I mean when I say if you do not have a full understanding of how a thing works you limit yourself to how it can best serve you. Many of God's children have a limited understanding of wisdom and the many ways wisdom is instrumental to their lives.

You cannot fully benefit from something without first knowing all that it encompasses. How many times have you heard a person speak and say he or she spoke words of wisdom, or you've witnessed someone manage a demanding situation that caused you to say the person used a lot of wisdom in managing the situation. Many times, people tend to limit the acts of wisdom solely to how a person speaks or responds in crucial moments, however, there are many factors to wisdom. If you and I limit wisdom to merely these two components, the other areas of our lives that God intended for wisdom to aid us will go unassisted; we therefore become the reason wisdom eludes us, essentially robbing you and I of its power to contribute to our lives.

Wisdom is also the fear of God and its origin starts with God.

Proverbs 9:10 (KJV) 10
The fear of the LORD is the beginning of wisdom: and the knowledge of the holy is understanding.

The fear of God is the foundation or the start to real, authentic wisdom. How you start a thing is important to its outcome or well-being; whether it's a relationship, a business adventure or a building. This matters because it can affect other things along the way that are vital to the success of whatever it is you are building. Wisdom starts with an honorable relationship with God; one that recognizes God as Holy and Supreme more than anything and anyone. This is where wisdom begins. How you start something determines how well you finish or if you finish at all. Sprint runners understand the importance of a good start. The position of their Hands and feet must be precisely positioned in order to prevent any costly mistakes. The slightest mistake can cause a delay in how fast they are able to run. This minor yet critical start is vital to the outcome of a sprinters race. The better the runner starts, the better chance they have of winning the race. Their goal is to win, but a bad start guarantees them an absolute loss. You're not convinced, here's another example.

Likewise, construction workers understand the importance of a sturdy foundation. If you know anything about the construction of a house, you know the first element laid is the foundation. The foundation is the base or the start of a new home under construction. Before the roof, exteriors walls, windows or doors can go in, the foundation must be poured. The foundation provides support needed to distribute the load. The absence of a quality foundation could be the downfall of the entire house; after all, no house can stand on a weak foundation. I have never seen a house built without the foundation first being poured. Being that the foundation is what holds everything together, I can say without contradiction that it's the most significant part of any building. Just like the sprinters start is key to them having a successful race and the foundation of a house is essential to whether it stands or crumbles, the fear of God is the start to you and I ever even pursing wisdom.

The Hebrew word for fear is Yārē'. It involves two different meanings. One as being afraid; our English definition and understanding of the word fear. It also means reverence, involving a person in an exalted position. This is when someone recognizes the power and position of the individual revered and gives him or her prosper respect. (Vines Expository Dictionary)

In Genesis 32:11 (NLT2) Jacob says this; "O LORD, please rescue me from the hand of my brother, Esau. I am afraid that he is coming to attack me, along with my wives and children."

Jacob and Esau were not on good terms as Esau hated Jacob for stealing his blessing which Esau felt belonged to him. Esau in his heart wanted to kill Jacob. Jacob had the type of fear as defined by the English definition. You see this same Hebrew word for fear in Gen 22:12 when the angel of the Lord spoke these words to Abraham.

And he said, lay not thine hand upon the lad, neither do thou anything unto him: for now, I know that thou <u>fearest</u> God, seeing thou hast not withheld thy son, thine only *son* from me. Genesis 22:12 (KJV)

When Abraham chose to obey God when he was asked to sacrifice his own son, he demonstrated not only his love and dedication to God, but also his heart for God. God knew, in that moment there was nothing Abraham would withhold from him. Abraham showed God through his obedience how much he trusted and reverenced God. This must be the kind of fear we demonstrate to God; the kind Abraham had."

God does not want His children to have the kind of fear Jacob had for Esau. You can't have or build a healthy relationship with someone you are afraid of. You won't spend long amounts of time with the person, talk with them often, or ask them for anything when you are fearful of them. The other side of being in a fearful relationship is being in a loving relationship. A relationship where you feel loved and valued is one where you can't spend enough time with the person. You enjoy it so much that you go out of your way to be with the person. When you can't be with them, you call them just so you can hear their voice, that's just how vital the relationship is to you. It's a relationship that consists of not only a great deal of love, but great honor and respect also. If you don't have a great deal of respect, honor and reverence of God, you won't have a healthy relationship with God; preventing you from ever obtaining the kind of wisdom God wants you to have. Your reverence and devotion to God is critical to the role God plays in your life. God needs to know that His children hold Him in highest esteem in their lives, it is the determining factor to us having all our needs met.

While doing my research for this book I came across this quote from Lyman Abbott an American Congregationalist Theologian.

> *"To me Christ is less an object of knowledge than of simple reverence and love. I know no reverence that goes beyond the reverence I give to Him; no love I ever knew goes beyond the love I want to offer Him; there is no loyalty that transcends the loyalty I wish to pay Him."*
> —Lyman Abbott

What a powerful statement and testimony. I hold Christ in the Highest regard above everyone else in my life. Why should we *expect* anything from God if we fail to give Him the one thing, He most deserves. The world comes with its own challenges, in fact; Jesus called them "trials and tribulations." How we make it through them depends on our stance towards God. It's never too late to start doing something right that you have been doing wrong, if you are reading this book and you know your reverence of God is not what it should be and what He absolutely requires, begin anew today. These were the instructions given to the children of Israel by Moses regarding God. They are words we are required to and should strive to live by also.

Deuteronomy 10:20 (KJV)
[20] Thou shalt fear (reverence) the LORD thy God; him shalt thou serve, and to him shalt thou cleave, and swear by his name.

Tell God how you have taken Him for granted, apologize and honor Him in the way He deserves. He proved Himself by showing how much He loves His children from the start without ever having received anything from us when He gave us His only begotten son to pay our sin debt.

I want the blessings of the Lord upon my life daily, and I'm certain you want the same also. It starts with our reverence of God.

Psalm 111:10 (MSG)
[10] The good life begins in the fear of GOD— Do that and you'll know the blessing of GOD.

Chapter Two
How To Obtain Wisdom

Proverbs 2:6 (KJV)
⁶ For the LORD giveth wisdom: out of his mouth cometh knowledge and understanding.

James 1:5 (NLT2)
⁵ If you need wisdom, ask our generous God, and he will give it to you. He will not rebuke you for asking.

In James, wisdom is sourced from the Greek word Sopho. It speaks to two kinds of wisdom, worldly wisdom and Godly wisdom. I explained the two types of wisdom in chapter one. Let's look again at the definition of both.

Worldly Wisdom: *self-confidence and self-knowledge and understanding which comes through human sources.*

Godly Wisdom: *an enlightenment or insight of knowledge and understanding that cannot be attained through any human source; it is a*

Spiritual level of dimension that allows the believer to have awareness from God's perspective.

The wisdom James speaks of that the believer should ask of God is of course Godly wisdom; understanding, discernment and insight, which is gained through the Spirit realm. Everything in the Spirit realm comes by way of God. This means in order to operate in Godly wisdom there first has to be a spiritual connection to God. Remember Proverbs 9:10 (KJV) The fear of the LORD *is* the beginning of wisdom: and the knowledge of the holy *is* understanding. When you are not properly connected things won't work as they should. Think of it this way; my house is wired for power, but without a direct connection to Florida Power & Light, my local utility company, not one single appliance or light fixture will come on in my house. Despite the expertise of the electricians who installed the wiring in my home, they were unable to activate any power without directly collaborating with FPL.

Some homes today use solar panels as a means to help keep one's utility cost down, but without the use of daylight, a source of energy, divinely created by God, solar panels are useless. **Genesis 1:3 (NLT2)** [3] Then God said, "Let there be light," and there was light. **Genesis 1:5 (NLT2)** [5] God called the light "day." The wiring in my house and the solar panel is both useless without the proper connection to the source needed to give it power. Your connection to God is equally critical to you obtaining wisdom from God. God is the power source who is the determining factor to how effectively we live out our lives for Him. Since we understand Godly wisdom entails, understanding, discernment and insight, gained through the Spirit realm, we can also conclude that wisdom is not a trait you got from your parents. It is not something you can get on your own, it's not something you can function in without God's assistance. It is the supernatural power of God working through you and I to perform at a level of capacity that helps you and I achieve God connected results we could never accomplish without Him. God results are all about what God wants, what He endeavors to accomplish.

Godly wisdom is never about what you and I want or what you and I think is best. Godly wisdom is never about the outcome we desire, but the outcome God has determined is best for the situation. It never includes yours or my will, it only involves the will of God. Our will, which revolves around our flesh, gives no consideration to anything or anyone else's wishes, it seeks to solely satisfy its own needs, it is self-driven 24/7. It will never desire the things of God or seek to please God. Godly wisdom does not involve selfishness. Your flesh is egocentric. It craves what it wants; when it wants it; and how it wants it. Godly wisdom understands there are moments in life where everything can't be about self. It is not an easy thing to resist your flesh. Your flesh is in constant communication with you 24/7. It has been with you since the very day you were born, it's used to having its way because it never had to contend with opposition until Holy Spirit moved in. Now there is this battle going on inside of you and both are fighting for control.

Jesus had to contend with His flesh. There was a war going on between Jesus' flesh and Spirit when Jesus was in the garden of Gethsemane.

Matthew 26:39 (KJV)
³⁹ And he went a little further, and fell on his face, and prayed, saying, O my Father, if it be possible, let this cup pass from me. This was Jesus's flesh talking, His flesh did not want to endure the cross. His flesh wanted to avoid the agony and pain of the cross, preventing Him from doing His Father's will.

Galatians 5:17 (KJV)
¹⁷ For the flesh lusteth against the Spirit, and the Spirit against the flesh: and these are contrary the one to the other: so that ye cannot do the things that ye would.

When you are Spirit led you ignore what your flesh wants and instead follow the dictates of the Spirit, which always pleases and does the will of God.

Let's face it, there are times when decisions must be made, decisions that are not always easy, decisions that are at times downright difficult. None I dare say as difficult as the one Jesus made in the Garden of Gethsemane. Still, we at times feel an enormous amount of weight in having to make them. It is our spiritual connection to God that helps guide you and I beyond what our flesh dictates, in order that we may fulfill the will of God. Only the Spirit could help Jesus say, "nevertheless not as I will, but as thou wilt" **(Mathew 5:26[b]).** Adversity no doubt can be painful, however God can use them to supply us with what we need to fulfill His will for our lives. It is our spiritual connection that helps push us past the pain and focus on the greater need. I cannot overstate the importance of your Spiritual connection to God. No one 's voice or desires, even your own is more important than God's. Imagine had Jesus made the decision to not endure the pain of the cross and instead gave into what His flesh wanted. What if He decided the cup was indeed too bitter? I for one am forever grateful that He did not operate out of His flesh but instead His Spirit.

The flesh only focuses on the cost and not the loss. My husband and I once made a decision that cost us more than it should have because we operated in our flesh instead of listening to and trusting the wisdom of God. Anytime you do what is best over what God knows and says is best, you are operating in your own wisdom which always leads to a greater loss. A many of bad decisions have been made because there are those who would rather forgo, pain and evade loss, failing to realize they loss the moment they disobeyed God. We did not want to lose the money we'd already invested, so we trusted our decision making over that of God's. Unfortunately for us we discovered later that, the wisdom of God is far greater than ours. In all honesty we already knew that; we just didn't want to incur the loss. God was advising us to take the smaller loss now because He knew there will be a greater loss later if we went ahead with our own plans. God knew in advance what we did not foresee happening later.

Remember Godly wisdom is insight imparted to us to navigate situations where we lack clarity. When relied upon, it provides us with the best possible answer for the situation. You might say well why didn't God just tell us how things would turn out from the start; it could have saved us a lot of hardship. Yes, it would have been nice to know the outcome in advance, however; there are no real lessons learned when you and I know the outcome beforehand.

During my childhood, my mom would tell my siblings and me if we had not completed our house chores by the time she returned home from work, we would face consequences .Her rationale for doing so was highly effective in ensuring the chores would be done, as we were motivated by fear of punishment if they were not. Since we did not want to be punished nor knew the severity of the punishment, we did what we were instructed to do. In all honesty, the penalty should not have been the primary motivator for completing our chores. Instead, we should have done them for several key reasons. Firstly, because she instructed us to; secondly, due to her authority as our parent; and thirdly, as an act of obedience.

God holds the highest position of authority in the believer's life; His instructions are extremely important. They matter, from the smallest of details to the greatest. If He says go, you get up and go. It would be wonderful if more of God's children were like Abram/Abraham. He just trusted God. Let's look at these two accounts of Abram/Abraham's complete compliance.

Genesis 12:1-4 (NLT2)
¹ The LORD had said to Abram, "Leave your native country, your relatives, and your father's family, and go to the land that I will show you.

² I will make you into a great nation. I will bless you and make you famous, and you will be a blessing to others.

³ I will bless those who bless you and curse those who treat you with contempt. All the families on earth will be blessed through you."

⁴ So Abram departed as the LORD had instructed, and Lot went with him. Abram was seventy-five years old when he left Haran.

Genesis 22:1-3 (NLT2)
¹ Some time later, God tested Abraham's faith. "Abraham!" God called. "Yes," he replied. "Here I am."

² "Take your son, your only son—yes, Isaac, whom you love so much—and go to the land of Moriah. Go and sacrifice him as a burnt offering on one of the mountains, which I will show you."

³ The next morning Abraham got up early. He saddled his donkey and took two of his servants with him, along with his son, Isaac. Then he chopped wood for a fire for a burnt offering and set out for the place God had told him about.

Few if any could do what Abram/Abraham did. Too many of His children want all the details before they move. God does not have to give us all the details, if He did some of His children still wouldn't go. If God has to give you all the details that means you do not trust God. God knows what He is doing. Remember He is the all-knowing, all wise God, what better person to trust with your life than Him. His children at times put their trust in other things more than God, such as our Jobs, our wealth and our own intellect. Proverbs and Jeremiah state this:

Proverbs 3:5-6 (KJV)

⁵ Trust in the LORD with all thine heart; and lean not unto thine own understanding. ⁶ In all thy ways acknowledge him, and he shall direct thy paths.

Jeremiah 9:23-24ᵃ (KJV)

²³ Thus saith the LORD, Let not the wise man glory in his wisdom, neither let the mighty man glory in his might, let not the rich man glory in his riches: ²⁴ But let him that glorieth glory in this, that he understandeth and knoweth me.

Even when you are doing a good thing you still need the wisdom of God leading you.

Acts 16:6-7 (NLT2)

⁶ Next Paul and Silas traveled through the area of Phrygia and Galatia, because the Holy Spirit had prevented them from preaching the word in the province of Asia at that time.

⁷ Then coming to the borders of Mysia, they headed north for the province of Bithynia, but again the Spirit of Jesus did not allow them to go there.

Paul and Silas were forbidden by the Spirit to go to the province of Bithynia. Scripture does not tell us why. Here we see Paul and Silas on a mission to teach the gospel, nonetheless the Spirit forbade them to go. Like I said God does not have to give you and I any of the details on a command. He knows the beginning and the end of things, we do not. We only know what's in front of us. We live in the right now; we are not capable of knowing what will happen 1) second or 1 minute from now, only God knows. All God wants from His children is trust.

When you trust God's directives, you never have to live with regrets. When you operate in the wisdom of God there are never mishaps, sorrows or feelings of misgivings after the fact. God is incapable of making bad or wrong decisions. All we have to do is follow His lead and **all** things will work out the way they are meant to. We can make all kind of excuses as to why we didn't do something, however; there is never an excuse you or I can give that is suitable or satisfactory for us disobeying the voice of God, NEVER! There is this man in the bible who clearly did not understand the importance of God's voice in his life, he not once, but twice disobeyed God and it cost him greatly! Go with me to I Samuel 15.

1 Samuel 15:10-11 (KJV)
[10] Then came the word of the LORD unto Samuel, saying,

[11] It repenteth me that I have set up Saul to be king: for he is turned back from following me, and hath not performed my commandments. And it grieved Samuel; and he cried unto the LORD all night.

1 Samuel 15:16-22 (KJV)
[16] Then Samuel said unto Saul, Stay, and I will tell thee what the LORD hath said to me this night. And he said unto him, Say on.

[17] And Samuel said, When thou wast little in thine own sight, wast thou not made the head of the tribes of Israel, and the LORD anointed thee king over Israel?

[18] And the LORD sent thee on a journey, and said, Go and utterly destroy the sinners the Amalekites, and fight against them until they be consumed.

[19] Wherefore then didst thou not obey the voice of the LORD, but didst fly upon the spoil, and didst evil in the sight of the LORD?

[20] And Saul said unto Samuel, Yea, I have obeyed the voice of the LORD, and have gone the way which the LORD sent me, and have brought Agag the king of Amalek, and have utterly destroyed the Amalekites.

[21] But the people took of the spoil, sheep and oxen, the chief of the things which should have been utterly destroyed, to sacrifice unto the LORD thy God in Gilgal.

²² And Samuel said, Hath the LORD as great delight in burnt offerings and sacrifices, as in obeying the voice of the LORD? Behold, to obey is better than sacrifice, and to hearken than the fat of rams.

Saul had two problems, one being his disobedience to God and the other being, his willingness to listen to the people rather than God. ***1 Samuel 15:24 (KJV)*** *²⁴ And Saul said unto Samuel, I have sinned: for I have transgressed the commandment of the LORD, and thy words: because I feared the people, and obeyed their voice.* As I stated, there is never a reason to disobey God. Fear of something or someone is never a valid reason to disobey God. God possesses the capability to handle any obstacle with which you are faced. I'm certain King Saul could have never anticipated Samuel speaking these words to him. "For rebellion *is as* the sin of witchcraft, and stubbornness *is as* iniquity and idolatry. *Because thou hast rejected the word of the LORD, he hath also rejected thee from* being *king."* ***1 Samuel 15:23 (KJV)*** Look at what it cost King Saul, his reign as King.

Do you ever sit down and think about what a simple act of disobedience to God could potentially cost you. I can tell you this, it certainly won't be something with which you are happy. There were a few times I considered doing something my mom said not to do; but then I imagined the thoughts of what she would do to me if I did, those thoughts changed my mind. Sometimes we disobey God because we don't think first, we don't reflect on what God said, nor the disappointment it causes God.

1 Samuel 15:10-11 (KJV) *¹⁰ Then came the word of the LORD unto Samuel, saying,* ¹¹ *It repenteth me that I have set up Saul to be king: for he is turned back from following me, and hath not performed my commandments. And it grieved Samuel; and he cried unto the LORD all night.*

God was sorrowful that He had chosen Saul to be king. God is grieved and hurt by our disobedience. We may not think we are disobedient if we leave out one minor detail, but we are. Details are important to God, all of what God says to do is vital. Leaving one Amalekite alive meant the children of Israel would have to continuously deal with them. This oversight may not have meant much to the children of Israel then, but it would later if left undealt with. God gives us specific directives now, so we do not have to contend with the fallout later. Put your thoughts on the matter aside and follow His lead so you do not end up battling the same old trouble over and over again.

Let me share something you may or may not be aware of. God's relinquishment of the Kingdom from Saul didn't start when he disobeyed God in 1 Samuel 15. The kingdom was being stripped from Saul back in 1 Samuel 13 when Saul first disobeyed God. Let's look 1 Samuel 10:8 and 1 Samuel 13:8-14.

1 Samuel 10:8 (KJV)
8 And thou shalt go down before me to Gilgal; and, behold, I will come down unto thee, to offer burnt offerings, and to sacrifice sacrifices of peace offerings: seven days shalt thou tarry, till I come to thee, and shew thee what thou shalt do.

1 Samuel 13:8-14 (KJV)
8 And he tarried seven days, according to the set time that Samuel had appointed: but Samuel came not to Gilgal; and the people were scattered from him.

9 And Saul said, Bring hither a burnt offering to me, and peace offerings. And he offered the burnt offering.

10 And it came to pass, that as soon as he had made an end of offering the burnt offering, behold, Samuel came; and Saul went out to meet him, that he might salute him.

¹¹ And Samuel said, What hast thou done? And Saul said, Because I saw that the people were scattered from me, and that thou camest not within the days appointed, and that the Philistines gathered themselves together at Michmash;

¹² Therefore said I, The Philistines will come down now upon me to Gilgal, and I have not made supplication unto the LORD: I forced myself therefore, and offered a burnt offering.

¹³ And Samuel said to Saul, Thou hast done foolishly: thou hast not kept the commandment of the LORD thy God, which he commanded thee: for now would the LORD have established thy kingdom upon Israel for ever.

¹⁴ But now thy kingdom shall not continue: the LORD hath sought him a man after his own heart, and the LORD hath commanded him to be captain over his people, because thou hast not kept that which the LORD commanded thee.

One act of disobedience could potentially cost you the thing you can never get back. Adam and Eve never entered the Garden of Eden again; they were thrown out of (Paradise). The slightest disregard of something God tells you to do could be a matter of life or death, wealth or poverty, a joy or heartache, we just don't know. The severity of discounting the importance of God's wisdom in our life on any matter can not only disrupt our lives but potentially forfeit future blessings God wants you and I to have. I'm not saying God will stop blessing us all together, what I'm saying is there are positions God may not allow you to stay in, places you may never be able to return to, losses you may never recover. from. We must be in union with God not man to accomplish His directives. I'm not suggesting that alignment with your leader is not necessary to achieve the vision. However, adhering to God's instructions should take precedence. A God -driven vision can still be accomplished despite disgruntle members. What God will not accept is disobedience to Him to appease anyone. Remember what happened to Moses.

Numbers 20:10-12 (KJV)

[10] And Moses and Aaron gathered the congregation together before the rock, and he said unto them, Hear now, ye rebels; must we fetch you water out of this rock?

[11] And Moses lifted up his hand, and with his rod he smote the rock twice: and the water came out abundantly, and the congregation drank, and their beasts also.

[12] And the LORD spake unto Moses and Aaron, Because ye believed me not, to sanctify me in the eyes of the children of Israel, therefore ye shall not bring this congregation into the land which I have given them.

In his frustration with the children of Israel Moses struck the rock instead of speaking to it. That act of disobedience left him missing the promise land because he disobeyed a God directive. One mistake could be the biggest and most costly mistake of your life, why risk it. You and I don't know the cost of disobedience to God; He does, that being the case, it's best to simply obey!

Proverbs 4:20-22 (KJV)

[20] My son, attend to my words; incline thine ear unto my sayings. 21 Let them not depart from thine eyes; keep them in the midst of thine heart.

[22] For they are life unto those that find them, and health to all their flesh.

Chapter Three
The Character of Wisdom

While doing research for this book, one of the things I like to do is look at the meanings of words. In doing so I ran across this insightful definition for the word character in the Practical Bible Illustration. PBI defines character as this:

"Character is an engraving; something carved or inscribed in a man's nature; it is the potential fact about the man, the inmost truth of him written upon his personality; which on the whole his fellow men can read and perceive accurately, and from which God at last will judge him." (Practical Bible Illustrations)

I found this definition to be intriguing. Two words stood out to me: the words engraving and potential. If you know anything about engravings you understand that an engraving is something that is stitched, embossed or carved into a piece of material, such as fabric, wood or metal. When an image is engraved into something, the only way to remove it would be by way of sanding. The deeper the engraving the longer the sanding process will take to remove it. A minor scratch on a wooden table can be removed by light sanding using sandpaper, however; a deep scratch may take a sanding machine to remove it.

Why am I going on with engraving and sanding, you might ask. The reasons being twofold. First, to provide a deeper understanding of the effort required to remove engraved elements and secondly, to highlight the similarities between the two words: character and engraving. Your character, like an engraving, leaves an indelible imprint in the minds of people which is not easily removed. If you leave a good impression on people that's fine, you have nothing to worry about, however; if you leave a negative impression in the minds of people then there is reason for concern.

It is common for individuals to dwell on negative experiences longer than positive ones. This tendency can shape the way people react to events in their relationships. When conflict arises, instead of resolving the current issue, one or both parties may recall a past flaw, serving as a reminder that the individual is still perceived as having not changed.

Even when a person has made a genuine effort and visible change in their character, there will be someone who will have difficulty believing the person has grown and is no longer the same individual they once knew. This one fact alone gives weight to why living a life of godly character is so important, first impressions can be lasting impressions.

PBI also stated character is the potential fact about a man. Potential speaks to the possibility of something or someone. Oxford Languages Dictionary describes potential as this:" having or exhibiting the capacity to become or develop into something in the future." This implies that certain behaviors both positive and negative being demonstrated are indicative of one's potential future behavior. Although not definitive it does imply the possibility of future patterns of behavior, why? Because habits are being formed. As my husband would say, "Anything you do once; you have the potential of repeating." There is no need to change good behavior, however; if the behavior is negative and destructive, you and I need to give immediate attention to it. Anything you do repetitively speaks to it potentially being a permanent part of your character. It won't be as easy to eliminate unruly behavior from your life as you think, because "Old habits die hard" meaning, it's hard to stop doing things one has been doing for a long time. Try taking a bottle or pacifier from a baby who's been sucking on it for 12 months. It won't be an easy adjustment to living without one because the baby has become accustomed to having it. I'm here to tell you, get ready for some restless nights.

When Carlos Jr turned one year old, my husband and I made a joint decision to eliminate bottles and pacifiers from his routine. Although we were resolute, Jr's resolve differed. He was willing to part ways with the bottle, but relinquishing the pacifier proved more challenging. ok with not having a bottle, but he was unwilling to part ways with his pacifier. He may have been thinking you can take one but not both. After a few nights of realizing he was not going to sleep without his pacifier and understanding we needed our sleep, we quickly found out we were going to have to manage this situation differently.

We decided he could only give him his pacifier during bedtimes; afternoon naps and when he was down for the night. Eventually we were able to wean him off of it, but it took some time. It required us to adhere to and to exercise patience. It was unreasonable to expect him to quit doing something he has become accustomed to doing instantaneously.

I am a coffee drinker, I mean seriously; I don't just drink coffee occasionally, I drink coffee every day; twice a day and sometimes three times a day. Some years ago, some brilliant person came out with the

Keurig coffee maker. When I open my eyes each morning the first thing, I do is say good morning God, thank you for another day and make my way to my Keurig coffee maker. My Keurig only made my love of drinking coffee worse, because now I can make coffee as often as I like in less time and effort. I wasn't always a habitual coffee drinker. In the past, I rarely drank coffee, less than ten cups a year. Over time I have developed a habit that is not easy to break.

Truth be told, I am not just a coffee drinker, I am a coffee addict! If you know like I know addictions are hard to break no matter what the addiction is. One can be addicted to shopping, smoking, eating, it doesn't matter about the addiction. If you ever make the decision to stop, you will see it won't be as easy as you think. This is why it is so important to recognize and deal with ungodly characteristics as quickly as possible. If we do not, we run the risk of it becoming a stronghold in our lives that is difficult to break free from. Notice I did not say it would be impossible, I said it would be difficult easy especially if it's something you've been doing for an exceptionally long time.

Godly character is something we must practice demonstrating every day of our lives; because as I've stated, it plays a key role in the impact you and I will have on others. Your character will do two things; draw people to you; or move them away from you! Let's be real, some individuals will require substantial evidence to be convinced you have moved past previous negative behavior regardless of your efforts, because they just refuse to believe you have changed. Unfortunately, there is nothing you can do about these kinds of people.

All the miracles Jesus performed, all the teaching all the love and compassion He demonstrated, there were still those who rejected Him, criticized Him and hated Him while doing only that which was good. In spite of how people treated Him while He walked the earth, Jesus continued demonstrating the loving, compassionate characteristics of His Father. Even after being whipped, hung on a cross, spat upon, pierced in the side, having a thorn of crown thrust upon His head and given vinegar to quench his thirst, Jesus said *"Father forgive them for they know not what they do". (Luke23:34)"* Jesus always demonstrated His Father's godly character. Scripture tells us in Acts 8:32 (KJV), He was led as a sheep to the slaughter; and like a lamb dumb before his shearer, so opened he not his mouth. Christ is the greatest example of the kind of godly character you and I are to demonstrate at all times, no matter what we face in life.

One evening as I was watching an episode of "The Crown" a young Queen Elizabeth II at the time was having a conversation with her grandmother who was once Queen. Still very new in her new role as head of state, the young Queen was struggling with the decision on whether to act regarding a major crisis in London. During her conversation with her grandmother Queen Elizabeth II stated these words, "it doesn't seem right to be head of state and do nothing at all. Her grandmother's response was this, "It is exactly right." Queen Elizabeth II then said; "surely doing nothing is no job at all." Her Grandmother's responded with these words, "to do nothing is the hardest job of all, and it will take every ounce of energy that you have." To be impartial is not natural, it's not human. People will always want you to smile, or to agree, or to frown, and the minute you do, you will have declared a position; a point of view and that is the one thing as sovereign you are not entitled to do. The less you do, or say or smile, the better."

I'm certain the former Queen was not implying Queen Elizabeth II take this stance on every issue. She herself was once Queen, I'm certain she watched her husband the former King in time past, have to make the same hard decisions her granddaughter is now having to make; whether to jump the gun and act, or hold off for now and do nothing.

Every situation does not require you and I to act. Some decisions require you and I to utilize wisdom in knowing when not to act. Sometimes doing nothing at all is the best response. As parents there are times we want to protect and rescue our children from everything. Sometimes getting involved does more harm than good, because as parents we at times fail to understand that some lessons are better learned by not always coming to our children's rescue. Again, I'm not saying this should always be our stance, I'm saying we should use wisdom in knowing when to get involved.

Jesus knew when to engage Himself in a matter and when to say nothing at all. It takes two to argue, so why engage; just because someone says or does something to hurt you, does not mean you have to retaliate. It's been said, "Character is not made in a crisis it is only exhibited." What do challenging circumstances reveal to others about you? Does it bring out the best in your or the worst in you? Retaliating oftentimes makes matters worse. Love on the other hand makes matters better. "For God so loved the word that He gave His only begotten son." John 3:16 By God demonstrating His love towards you and I, it made things better not worse!

Upon Jesus arrest hours before being crucified on the cross, He said this; *"Don't you realize that I could ask my Father for thousands of angels to protect us, and he would send them instantly?"* **Matthew 26:53 (NLT2)** In that moment Jesus did nothing. It was the hardest task He would have to do; in the midst of being beaten and crucified; He did nothing, he took the beating, something for you and me to remember when our Christianity is being attacked. Love is the best revenge. Christ showed the world that love always wins.

1 Peter 4:7-8 (NLT2)
⁷ The end of the world is coming soon. Therefore, be earnest and disciplined in your prayers.
⁸ Most important of all, continue to show deep love for each other, for love covers a multitude of sins.

We are living in a time where hate is evolving, and love is diminishing. Peter tells us, "Most important of all continue to show deep love." Love is what saved you and I, not hate. You and I will never undertake what Christ did for us on Calvary, nor will we be asked to, but we are asked to live a life of love. This is how Godly character conducts itself. As followers of Christ, we are called to be imitators of Him and must strive to walk in godly character always.

Ephesians 5:1-2 (NLT2)
¹ Imitate God, therefore, in everything you do, because you are his dear children.
² Live a life filled with love, following the example of Christ. He loved us and offered himself as a sacrifice for us, a pleasing aroma to God.

Scripture tells us we are to imitate Christ in everything we do! God's children at times are too easily offended. We lose it if someone says something that hurts our feelings or does something we do not like even when the persons actions did not directly involve us. You and I will have to deal with offenses until Christ returns, we can decide to be instruments that make matters better or make them worse. We can be instruments that give people hope or cause people more hurt. We can lead them to Christ or lead them astray. It isn't enough to say we are followers of Christ; it has to been seen. As I stated and will continue to remind you throughout this reading; wisdom is more than the words we speak and how well we judge a situation. Our actions speak volumes; they give a truer indication of the kind of person you and I say we are. Our mouths may speak one thing, but our actions will always tell the truth!

James 3:13 (MSG) *^{13} Do you want to be counted wise, to build a reputation for wisdom? Here's what you do: Live well, live wisely, live humbly. It's the way you live, not the way you talk, that counts. Talk is cheap!*

James 3:13 (KJV)
^{13} Who is a wise man and endued with knowledge among you? let him shew out of a good conversation his works with meekness of wisdom.

The word conversation in James has nothing to do with speech but your behavior. Let's look at this same verse in the New Living translation of the Bible.

James 3:13 (NLT2)
^{13} If you are wise and understand God's ways, prove it by living an honorable life, doing good works with the humility that comes from wisdom.

It's one thing to claim wisdom, but it's another to provide evidence of it. The old adage "talk is cheap" is true. We can't just talk about it we must be about it. You and I can scream to the roof tops we have the wisdom of God, but people typically judge based on demonstrated actions rather than claims. Scripture tells us there is a way wisdom behaves.

"If you are wise and understand God's ways, prove it by living an honorable life, doing good works with the humility that comes from wisdom. But if you are bitterly jealous and there is selfish ambition in your heart, don't cover up the truth with boasting and lying. <u>For jealousy and selfishness are not God's kind of wisdom. Such things are earthly, unspiritual, and demonic.</u> For wherever there is jealousy and selfish ambition, there you will find disorder and evil of every kind. But the wisdom from above is first of all pure. It is also peace loving, gentle at all times, and willing to yield to others.

It is full of mercy and the fruit of good deeds. It shows no favoritism and is always sincere. And those who are peacemakers will plant seeds of peace and reap a harvest of righteousness." (James 3:13-18 NLT)

In the book of James, you can clearly see that the wisdom from above speaks directly to one's actions. It is more than speaking wise words, it is more than judging or management of a situation. If we as children of God are going to bear witness that we indeed are children who operate in the wisdom of God, there must be evidence that is proven through our conduct and interactions with others.

James tells us of the two kinds of wisdom I spoke of in my introduction, earthy or worldly wisdom and Spiritual wisdom. In this particular passage of scripture, James is speaking to those who are teachers or desire to teach, but this is a rule for all of God's children to live by. James describes the behavior patterns of earthly wisdom; it is bitterly jealous (envy), has selfish ambition in one's heart and if that wasn't bad enough, he adds this, it unspiritual and demonic! The presence of these two things in one's life comes with disorder and evil of every kind; let that sink in for a moment. If this does not scare a person into wanting to rid themselves of this kind of behavior, I do not know what will.

Jealousy led Cain to kill his brother Abel. Jealousy led Joseph's brother to put him in a ditch, sell him into slavery and allow their father to believe his son was dead. Jealousy never leads to anything good. Jealousy can turn to hate, and hate can lead to murder if you do not get it under control. The thing you need to realize is you can't conqueror this on your own. Remember scripture defines earthly wisdom as demonic, which lets us know the only way to conquer the demonic is through the Spirit realm.

In Mark chapter 3 the teachers of the religious laws accused Jesus of being possessed by Satan; Jesus responded with these words "How can

Satan cast out Satan, a kingdom divided against himself will not stand. "Jesus had just cast a demon (representative of the strong man) out of a man that was mute. This is example of The Spirit overpowering the demonic. Do not fool yourself into thinking you can overpower demonic behavior on your own, you need the help of the Spirit realm to do so. The danger of trusting in earthly wisdom is to put your trust in a person who relies on their own knowledge and understanding. This person thinks they know all and know what best at all times. This kind of person feels no need to seek guidance from anyone else. This kind of person deceives themselves. Corinthians warns us.

1 Corinthians 3:18-20 (KJV)
[18] Let no man deceive himself. If any man among you seemeth to be wise in this world, let him become a fool, that he may be wise.

[19] For the wisdom of this world is foolishness with God. For it is written, He taketh the wise in their own craftiness.

[20] And again, The Lord knoweth the thoughts of the wise, that they are vain.

> Don't permit jealousy to dominate your life, deal with it the moment it rears its ugly head. James reminds us, concealing jealousy is not the solution. "Don't cover it up." Covers ups do just that, cover up what's really there. Anytime I gain weight and don't want my belly fat to show, I opt for a bigger top. I'm certain I'm not alone in this. Guess what, the belly fat is still there underneath that oversized garment. The answer to my problem is not to cover it up, the answer lies in shedding the excess weight. If I did nothing the situation would only get worse.
>
> There is a sure-fire way to know if you are behaving more like your Heavenly Father or more like the devil, I mean James did call jealousy and bitterness demonic; umm, who else do you know that operates in the demonic; that would be Satan. Do a daily inspection of yourself, if you find yourself behaving badly it's time to do a spiritual cleansing of oneself. Daily remind yourself of how James says true wisdom

behaves. *"But the wisdom from above is first of all pure. It is also peace loving, gentle at all times, and willing to yield to others. It is full of mercy and the fruit of good deeds. It shows no favoritism and is always sincere. And those who are peacemakers will plant seeds of peace and reap a harvest of righteousness."* (James 3:15-18 NLT)

Chapter Four
Listen Up

Proverbs 1:20-23 (NLT2)
[20] *Wisdom shouts in the streets. She cries out in the public square.*
[21] *She calls to the crowds along the main street, to those gathered in front of the city gate:*
[22] *"How long, you simpletons, will you insist on being simpleminded? How long will you mockers relish your mocking? How long will you fools hate knowledge?*
[23] *Come and listen to my counsel. I'll share my heart with you and make you wise.*

How well do you listen? To the one who listens well, there is an abundance of knowledge and understanding waiting for them. Our listening skills will influence how much knowledge and understanding we gain. Our ability to listen is crucial in our walk with God. I'm willing to go out on a limb and say many people will say they are great listeners. Yet if you ask those same individuals about mistakes they've made, many will admit they failed to use wisdom. What they are really saying is they did not pay attention to wisdom even when it was available to them. It is usually after a mishap we realize wisdom was trying to guide our decisions differently, we simply were not listening. The significance of listening often becomes clear only after we fail to listen.

In order to be a great listener, you have to do it with intention. You cannot be preoccupied with other concerns; your full focus has to be on what is being presently said. How many times did you believe you were actively listening, only to discover that you had in fact missed a substantial portion of the conversation. It was not until you were asked to recap the discussion that you realized your listening skills were not as effective as you had assumed.

When my daughter Andrea was young, approximately three years of age, I recall instructing her to go retrieve a particular item from her room. She would happily respond with a big smile on her face, ok mommy. However, a few seconds later she would come back and ask, mommy what did you ask me to get. In that moment even though she heard me, I knew she was not really listening to me. She would be standing right in front of me as I was speaking to her and would still ask mommy what did you say? Her little mind would be somewhere else. I would ask my husband, have you noticed that Andrea occasionally appears to forger something you instruct her to get?

We never for one minute thought Andrea had a hearing problem, nor an understanding problem, but she did have what's known as Pseudo; mindless or passive listening. This was evident because when my husband or I informed her that we were taking her somewhere she desired to go or buy her something, she could recall every word we spoke in detail. Mindless listening involves faking attention to appear attentive while your mind is elsewhere. Mindless listening also involves only listening for what you want to hear. Passive listening is when you hear information without fully engaging, responding or processing it. The difference is, she was more engaged when she felt what we were saying benefitted her, whereas when it did not, she gave less attention to our words. My baby was playing us like a fiddle at a young age, lol. If you have never heard that expression, it means tricking us. Say this to yourself, say it loudly; and say it with conviction. <u>Wisdom's Voice Is Always Relevant;</u> never forget this.

If you and I wish to avoid making repeated mistakes and wish to live our lives in the manner God intended for us, we will have to adopt the same mindset as those individuals had in the renowned 1970's EF Hutton commercial, "When EF Hutton talks, people listen." Don't be so busy that you do not have time to listen to wisdom's voice.

Earlier in the book I spoke of a time my husband and I moved on something, we clearly knew we should not have. We didn't listen because we were determined to get what we wanted. How costly that mistake was. In that moment we failed to understand the no was beneficial for our wellbeing. When we pause and choose to follow wisdom's guidance, even if it challenges our desires, we open ourselves to outcomes that lead to our highest good and when we do not it leads to the worst outcome imaginable.

Spiritual wisdom is always beneficial to our lives; Spiritual wisdom sometimes speaks things to us we do not want to hear; knowledge we do not agree with or like. The thing we need to remember is of wisdom never gives us bad advice. Like it or not, agree with it or not, wisdom never misleads us. Upon becoming King, Solomon asked the Lord for wisdom. *"Give therefore thy servant an understanding heart to judge thy people, that I may discern between good and bad"* **1 Kings 3:9 (KJV)**.

Not soon after this prayer, one of Solomon's first tests was to figure out who was the rightful mother of a child as two harlots claimed belonged to them. One woman had accidently rolled over on her child while sleeping thus killing the child. She then switched babies while the other woman slept and claimed the living baby as hers. Wisdom would have Solomon tell the two women, we will divide the child in two with a sword giving half to one and half to the other; sounds crazy right. However, the truth was revealed when the woman whose child it was chose to allow the child to live rather than die to have what was rightfully hers. In that moment Solomon knew who the real mother of the child was without having to do harm to the child. I'd like to think the child's biological mother exercised wisdom also; by her willingness to spare the child's life, allowing even if not in her care.

Wisdom always leads to truth, even when what wisdom instructs us to do makes no sense at all. We must still listen and follow its leading even when hesitant. I'd rather make a hesitant move than to not move at all. Remember the first step to wisdom is asking! Asking let's God know you trust His knowledge over your own. Feelings of reservations may come but do not allow those feelings to prevent you from trusting wisdoms guidance. Had Solomon not asked God for wisdom who knows how things would have turned out. It's when we think we know everything that we find out we know extraordinarily little and what great fools we are. Socrates said this; "The wisest man is the one who admits he knows nothing." Wouldn't you rather be like Solomon, at the start of your walk with God relying completely upon Him to help with your day-to-day decisions and encounters you face in life. Have you ever asked yourself how much farther along would I be had I sought God's wisdom from the start? You are not alone and it's never too late to correct bad judgment.

Proverbs 1:20-23 (NLT2)
[20] *Wisdom shouts in the streets. She cries out in the public square.*

²¹ She calls to the crowds along the main street, to those gathered in front of the city gate:

²² "How long, you simpletons, will you insist on being simpleminded? How long will you mockers relish your mocking? How long will you fools hate knowledge?

²³ Come and listen to my counsel. I'll share my heart with you and make you wise.

We gather several things from Proverbs chapter one about wisdom. **1) Wisdom makes her voice known by calling out to those who will stop what they are doing and take the time to listen to her.** Wisdom is portrayed as actively seeking out those who need her, emphasizing that understanding and discernment are available to all who are willing to listen. Wisdom does not have to be a stranger in the life of the believer, nor does wisdom want to. A stranger is someone you do not know or is unfamiliar with; Wisdom wants to be an integral part of your life, not a stranger. Wisdom is only a stranger to the person who is too busy to engage or listen. When babies cry, they cry to get their parents attention. The louder and more intense the cry becomes, the sooner they require their parents attention. Wisdom is shouting loudly to get folks attention, a particular class of people.

2) Wisdom is crying out to simpletons. ***Proverbs 1:22 (NLT)****"How long, you simpletons will you insist on being simpleminded."*

Simpleminded people, according to Proverbs, are people who are foolish. Cambridge dictionary definition of a fool is "someone who behaves silly or lacks good judgement. "You know there are believers that sometimes act foolishly and lack good judgment. This happens because they are ignorant of the way the wise behave. Now I know none of us like to be called a fool, but if we are honest with ourselves, we have all demonstrated foolish behavior at one time or another, it may have been something we said, did, or did not do, in that moment we were fools. Sometimes, it's not that we lack good judgment but that we deliberately rejected it. If we are honest, fools are people who reject what's right and good for them. I know believers who say they love God and say they want to live for God but will disregard God's way of doing things. We behave like fools anytime we reject God's methods.

Coming up as a child I would hear grown folk say I used to be young and dumb, what they were saying is they were young fools. My husband has a saying; "The only thing worse than a young fool is an old fool" I agree. If you're still acting foolish when you get old, that's intentional, you have made the decision to be a fool. We do not have to be life-long fools. The people in Proverbs were fools. Wisdom is crying out to get the simpleton's attention; Wisdom is in the street desiring to help the foolish. If Wisdom went out of the way to seek the foolish why wouldn't the spirit of wisdom seek out and speak to the believer. The Spirit is readily speaking, but are you open and positioned to hear.

3) Wisdom's voice was loud. This tells me it is impossible not to hear wisdom's voice. Anyone that knows me can attest to the fact that I talk loudly. Hard as I try, I do not have a low register, my whisper is even louder than most peoples. My G-baby who is 4 years of age will even tell me, Mima, you're too loud. It's not that we have a problem hearing; the problem at times is we disregard the voice of the spirit, or we are too distracted by other things to hear. As I stated I'm a loudmouth; go ahead and laugh I will not be offended. I once asked someone to do something, the person was in the house but across the way, I called out and they answered yes, I then asked them to do something in the same octave to make sure they heard me, the person never responded. I knew the individual had heard me, but they chose to ignore me because they did not want to do what I had asked.

Wisdom's voice escaped these people because they were preoccupied by other things happening around them. If they are out in the city they have to be there doing something. It is hard to hear when you are distracted. There have been times when my husband and I would be having a conversation, during the conversation he would call my name. The reason he would call my name was because he noticed my mind had gone elsewhere, I had become distracted and was no longer listening to what he was saying. It's not that Wisdom stops speaking, the problem is we've stopped listening. We've allowed something to take our attention away, so we miss what Wisdom has to say.

Wisdom wanted to pour into the minds of those who would listen. I'll say this again because it's worth repeating. *If Wisdom went out of her way to shout in the streets to the simple, how much more does The Spirit* want to communicate with you. The Spirit of Wisdom can scream to the rooftop, however; there are two things Wisdom will not do; make you listen and make you follow its instructions. It is up to you and me to listen; to lean in and hear what the Spirit has to say. It's on you and me to decide whether we will obey the Spirit's voice. Listening requires effort, hearing does not. You can hear someone speak but not be focused on what they are saying. My definition for focus is *Deliberate Intent!* Here are a few corresponding synonyms to further describe the word deliberate; *Meticulous, Calculated and Purposeful*. You can't miss Wisdom's voice when you go about listening, with this kind of intent.

When a person is deliberate in their actions towards what they are pursuing they are likely to get their desired outcome. My husband would tell people, "If my wife says she is going to do something you can count on her doing it because there is deliberate intent in doing it, and if she says she isn't going to do something you can count on her not doing it, because this too involves deliberate intent." We've all had at least one thing we desperately wanted to accomplish. The one thing I can tell you is this, you could not have accomplished the task without being deliberate in your actions towards reaching your desired goal.

When I want to lose weight, the first thing I know I must do is be intentional in how I go about it. I cannot just speak my weight lost into existence. I cannot go about my normal eating habits and think I'm going to reach my desired goal. I must go about doing things differently. What I eat, how much I eat, what time I eat, including what I drink, all play a vital role in reaching my goal. My exercise routine has to be considered; the amount of exercise I do, the amount of weight I lift is a factor, because too much weightlifting can actually cause you to gain weight instead of losing weight. All these changes are deliberate. If you desire to hear the spirit of God speak, it is essential to be deliberate in your intent to listen. If you are struggling to hear the spirit's voice, make a conscious decision to be more deliberate, purposeful and more intentional. The Holy Spirit offers valuable insights to share, but will not compel you to listen, it requires a deliberate choice by you to heed its guidance.

(Proverbs 1:23 (KJV)
[23] Turn you at my reproof: behold, I will pour out my spirit unto you, I will make known my words unto you. As I've stated Proverbs 23 shows Wisdom in the streets shouting to simpletons, fools. I also stated as God's children we have acted foolishly in some of our choices in life.

In **Proverbs chapter 1** we read that wisdom has the ability to alter and improve the foolish person's life. The message translation states it this way "I can revise your life." **(Proverbs 1:23[a])** Wisdom begins to correct bad judgment, bad decisions and unruly behavior. I do not know about you, but I've certainly needed Wisdom's voice to prevent me from making the same mistake twice, one time is enough! Who wants to do something stupid a second time, certainly not me and I hope not you either. Think of the times in your life when no one could tell you anything, especially in your teenage years. It's ok to admit it. What would be sad if you're still this way. None of us has all the answers, none of us are that smart regardless of how much education we have; we'll never be as smart as wisdom. We' will never know all there is to know about life or ourselves without wisdom's help.

"I'm ready to pour out my spirit on you; I'm ready to tell you all I know." **(Proverbs 1:23 MSG)**

All there is to know wisdom knows; there is absolutely nothing Spiritual Wisdom does not know! Spiritual Wisdom has the most comprehensive knowledge of everything. Spiritual Wisdom is information headquarters; the command post on all matters concerning you and me. What we should or should not do, where we or should not go, when to speak and when to keep silent, what is good for us and what is not. Every bit of information given is to improve our lives and we are better off for listening. Wisdom was willing and ready the people were not. In order for something to be received it must be accepted. Transference of information is not merely up to the Spirit; it is up to you and me to be accepting of the knowledge the Spirit wants to impart to us.

Transference rarely takes place unless two parties are agreeable. 2019 was the start of several years of a deadly infection called Covid-19 that was passed on to people unknowingly, a deadly infection people did not invite into their bodies, an infection folk did not even know they had until it was too late. This deadly infection entered their bodies without their knowledge; this is not that. You and I must be open to Spirits guidance. You can lock Spirit's voice out of your life, by lock I mean ignore its voice because the Spirit will not fight for entrance. Remember The Spirit does not force its way in. What wisdom does is speak to make its presence known and then leaves the decision up to us as to whether we choose to listen or simply ignore it's counsel.

You ever had something poured on you? The Greek word for pour is *Nāba;* one of the English words for *Nāba;* is gushing, we all know a gushing is not a small amount! What immediately came to mind was the image of water gushing out of a water fire hydrant or a football coach being drenched in Gatorade as his player pours it from a barrel like cooler on top of him. The Spirit wants to pour as much knowledge into you and I as we will allow. Since we are prone to make mistakes, it is to our advantage to embrace the knowledge wisdom has to offer us.

Proverbs also tells us this concerning something Wisdom and these people.; "**Proverbs 1:23 (MSG)** [23] About face! I can revise your life. Look, I'm ready to pour out my spirit on you; I'm ready to tell you all I know. These people would have had access to <u>all</u> wisdom's knowledge.

If you've ever encountered a nosey person, you are aware that nosey people want the 411 on everything and everyone. If you're sharing information with a nosey person and you are talking too fast, they will tell you, wait back up I missed that. They do not want to miss one single fact. Today I advise you to be nosey, get every ounce of knowledge and understanding you can. acquire; pose numerous questions, engage in daily conversations. I assure you wisdom will not object. Seek wisdom on every decision you have to make in life before you make it. Seek wisdom on what you do not know and especially on what you think you know because this is where we mostly mess up. We think we know all there is to know when in reality we do not. The Spirit does not mind sharing secrets with you and me. The Spirit has as much time as you are willing to dedicate; go ahead and pencil the Spirit in on your daily things to do list. I promise you it will not be wasted time.

Chapter Five
The Protection of Wisdom

Ecclesiastes 7:12 (AMP)
12 For wisdom is a defense even as money is a defense, but the excellency of knowledge is that wisdom shields and preserves the life of him who has it.

Proverbs 4:6 (NLT2)
6 Don't turn your back on wisdom, for she will protect you. Love her, and she will guard you.

When I think of the word protection, When I think of protection, I think of something that provides a form of security or safeguard. Safeguards prevent something bad from happening. Ecclesiastes tell us that Wisdom shields and preserves the life of him who has it. In the voice of Mr. T "I pity the fool" who decides to live their life without Wisdom's assistance. When my girls were babies, we would often visit a friend's home that had a pool. In order for them to enjoy being in the water and for us to feel more comfortable we would place these floaters on their arms that allowed them to float above the water. Even during times, we were in the pool with them, they had to have on floaters. Fast forward eight years later when my husband and I purchased our first home that came with a pool. The first thing we did was get our children swimming lessons. We did this for several reasons, (1) They were now too old for those arm floaters, they were no longer adequate enough to keep them above the water and (2) Swimming lessons provided the additional protection needed, as they were now of age where they could easily go outside at a moment's notice, and accidentally end up in the pool; so we needed to be certain of their safety. Here is something to think about; what are you still depending on to protect you that is not adequate enough?

My husband and I can swim but we are not great swimmers. He and I learned while we were at a fitness club from an old high school teacher of ours named Mr. Coats. Mr. Coats would see us in the pool, always near the shallow end of the water. One day he asked us why we were always at the shallow end of the pool. We responded, neither of us can swim. Mr. Coats taught the two of us how to stay afloat and swim on top of the water in about three or four lessons, sounds crazy: but it's the truth. The lessons were not even planned; they only happened because Mr. Coats happened to be at the fitness center the same days we were. The production of wisdom is available to every child of God. Wisdom is not to be sought after at the last minute or when a crisis appears, wisdom wants to play a pivotal role in our lives to avoid an unnecessary crisis. The time to teach our children swimming lessons was not after one of them was at risk of drowning but rather, before a tragic incident could have occurred, it was for prevention. Too often we wait until we are in the middle of a crisis to seek what God has made available to us all alone. Wisdom is there to assist you before, during and after trouble.

When a major earthquake hits what usually follows are aftershocks. Aftershocks are smaller earthquakes that usually follow in the same area.

If you know anything about earthquakes you know this, you also know the immediate threat is not over, so you don't go about your normal way of doing things, you are aware something could still be looming on the horizon. There are times that even after a crisis is over you still need wisdom on how to deal with what comes next.

As I stated, neither of us are great swimmers; we can hold our own, but do not ask us to save someone from drowning, we just know how to keep ourselves afloat. Of course, we would risk our lives to save our children, but what if they'd gone outside without us knowing. We could have kept life vests and other floating devices in the pool as an extra precaution, or placed that loud sounding alarm on the doors, however; that was not the best nor safest option. The situation is different than before; they now have Twenty-four-hour access to the pool; it was safer to teach them how to swim rather than risk something tragic happening. The swimming lessons provided the additional safeguard needed to protect them. Just like my husband and I put measures in place to protect the lives of our children, Wisdom is there to do the same for those who respect her voice. Wisdom enlightens us of things we have not even considered. There is a difference between your wisdom and the Spirit of Wisdom.

> *Remember **Godly Wisdom:** an enlightenment or insight of knowledge and understanding that cannot be attained through human source; it is a Spiritual level of dimension that allows the believer to have awareness from God's perspective. Spiritual wisdom illuminates your awareness of things you were totally in the dark about or had limited knowledge of.*

A boxer, no matter how skilled the boxer, is guaranteed to be defeated if he goes to a fight with his boxing gloves while his enemy has a magnum

Forty-seven, I think that a very crucial piece of information the boxer needs to be made aware of. This may be an over-the-top scenario, but this is exactly the kind of danger we put ourselves in we try to manage life's circumstances without Wisdom's insight. The enemy comes to kill, steal and destroy. Your adversary will utilize whatever means available to achieve this. How many times did you go it alone when you did not have to? We have a safeguard that we need to rely on for everything. I cannot think of a good enough reason to reject something that meant to provide protection.

7 Stabilizers of Wisdom

A stabilizer is a form of support, similar to that of a pillar or column. In construction columns or pillars are tall vertical structures of stone, wood or metal used as support for a building. They carry the weight needed to prevent the building from collapsing. Below I've compiled seven stabilizers of wisdom. Each serves a specific purpose that provides additional safeguards in the believer's life. I will not do a lengthy commentary on each of these stabilizers; However, I will give you some examples from scripture as to the importance of each of these support systems played in different situations. I do, however, recommend you do further research on each for yourself.

7 Stabilizers of Wisdom

- Fear of the Lord
- Instruction
- Knowledge
- Understanding
- Discretion
- Counsel
- Reproof

Fear of the Lord

Proverbs 9:10 (MSG)
¹⁰ Skilled living gets its start in the Fear-of-GOD, insight into life from knowing a Holy God.

Wisdom starts with an honorable relationship with God. It begins your awareness of who God is; Creator of all, Holy, Redeemer, and Just God to name a few. If you do not get this understanding from the onset, you will never obtain wisdom!

David is a fitting example of what it means to fear the Lord, I'm not speaking of fear in the sense of being afraid of God but rather your attitude, respect and obedience to God. There were times David could have killed Saul who certainly was determined to kill David, (see I Samuel 24:3-7 & 1 Samuel 26:8-12) however David's reverence for God dictated his behavior and actions towards God's anointed. David understood what God had given the throne to him even if Saul hadn't accepted it. You do not have to worry about your enemy when God gives you something. Just like God placed Saul in the position of Authority, God had the power to remove him.

Gideon is another excellent example we can look at. Gideon had an army of 32,00 but defeated his enemy with an army of three hundred. He could not have done this without being obedient to God's command. Fear of the Lord mandates our obedience even in times we are afraid. After Gideon has reduced his army to the three hundred, God instructed him to, he still was a little fearful but here is what God told Gideon.

Judges 7:10-15 (NLT2)
¹⁰ But if you are afraid to attack, go down to the camp with your servant Purah.

¹¹ Listen to what the Midianites are saying, and you will be greatly encouraged. Then you will be eager to attack." So Gideon took Purah and went down to the edge of the enemy camp.

¹² The armies of Midian, Amalek, and the people of the east had settled in the valley like a swarm of locusts. Their camels were like grains of sand on the seashore—too many to count!

¹³ Gideon crept up just as a man was telling his companion about a dream. The man said, "I had this dream, and in my dream a loaf of barley bread came tumbling down into the Midianite camp. It hit a tent, turned it over, and knocked it flat!"

¹⁴ His companion answered, "Your dream can mean only one thing—God has given Gideon son of Joash, the Israelite, victory over Midian and all its allies!"

¹⁵ When Gideon heard the dream and its interpretation, he bowed in worship before the LORD. Then he returned to the Israelite camp and shouted, "Get up! For the LORD has given you victory over the Midianite hordes!"

When God says He's got you, trust Him, you can totally rely on the words He speaks to you. Fear does not imply being afraid of God but rather walking in reverence of who He is. God is sovereign, He is supreme, He represents, your hope, strength and saving power, which is available to all who put their complete confidence in Him.

Instruction

Proverbs 2:1-5 (NLT2)
¹ My child, listen to what I say, and treasure my commands.
² Tune your ears to wisdom, and concentrate on understanding.
³ Cry out for insight, and ask for understanding.
⁴ Search for them as you would for silver; seek them like hidden treasures.

⁵ Then you will understand what it means to fear the LORD, and you will gain knowledge of God.

God's children do not have to live in ignorance. We have spiritual counsel that is eager to counsel and teach us on all the affairs of life. You need only be diligent, ask for wisdom's help and stay tuned into or sensitive to Wisdom's voice. It's not complicated, it's simply a matter of your doing what's necessary to acquire the help you need. Instruction is not to be looked at as simple rules but rather guidelines for living a purposeful life. Instructions often come with information that protects, guides, and informs. The only people who do not like instructions are people who think they know it all. There is no better instructor than that of our God!

Job 36:22 (NLT2)
²² "Look, God is all-powerful. Who is a teacher like him?

John 8:58 (NLT2)

Wisdom's voice will always instruct God's children down God's pathway in life. Wisdom's voice is God's voice just as Jesus was God in the earth.

James 1:5(KJV)
⁵⁸ Jesus answered, "I tell you the truth, before Abraham was even born, I AM!" Who else is known in the bible as "I AM". Why scripture tells us if you lack wisdom ask of God who giveth to all men liberally.

Abram later known as Abraham was a man of faith and a man who followed instruction. God told Abram to do two things that would be difficult for most people. **1.** leave their family and everything he knew and go to a place God would show him, **(See Genesis 12:1)**. **2.** Go offer up the promised son, both he and Sarah had long waited for. **(See Genesis 22:6)**. I cannot testify to the latter, but I can relate to leaving your family and everything I knew and moving to a place where my husband and I knew virtually no one. We knew one person in the entire city my husband was clear on where his next God assignment was. We moved but man did we cry in that hotel room like little children when reality kicked in that there was no going back. I can tell you this, we have not regretted following where God authorized us to go. **Trust in God will require you to move beyond your comfort zone!** Was it easy, no; but as my husband always says, "obedience is always better than any sacrifice we make on God's behalf."

Which leads to Abrahams second toughest decision. Let me correct that, it wasn't tough because scripture tells us Abraham rose early the next morning saddles his donkey and obeyed God. Let's be real some instructions from God are just downright hard, complexed and scary, but that is not a good enough reason to disobey God. Abraham showed us obedience to God's instructions do not have to be and aren't when we get our will out of the way and replace it with our faith. Proverbs 3:5-6 gives the believer clear instructions on how to be an obedience follower of God. Get your will out of the way!

Proverbs 3:5-6 (NLT2)
⁵ Trust in the LORD with all your heart; do not depend on your own understanding.
⁶ Seek his will in all you do, and he will show you which path to take.

Knowledge

Knowledge is divine power of insight that is given by way of the Spirit or God Himself. It cannot be attained through humanities limited comprehension. Godly Knowledge is a level of intelligence that is unmatched by any other source of communication. Man, alone does not have the capacity to reveal nor manage the unknow without the power of God operating in him. Sense the beginning man has always needed God voice and insight on how to live, that still holds true today. There in the midst of the Garden of Eden stood various trees, two of which included the tree of life and the tree of knowledge.

God gave Adam & Eve permission to eat from every tree in the garden except the tree of Knowledge.

There stood the tree of life to eat from, but they chose to eat from the one tree God said do not touch. From that moment life ended for man in the manner which God intended. Sin robbed us of eternal life with God, so Christ had to intervene to get man back in right standing with God. Man has to now choose between good and evil every day, struggling to make the right choices daily because they operated in what they thought to be a smart decision but was instead the most disastrous decision they would ever make. This lets us know man's wisdom is flawed, otherwise they would have trusted God's knowledge above their own and obeyed God. When we operate in the power of knowledge that God gives, it will produce God's will not our own.

Genesis 3:6 (NLT2)
⁶ The woman was convinced. She saw that the tree was beautiful and its fruit looked delicious, and she wanted the wisdom it would give her. So she took some of the fruit and ate it. Then she gave some to her husband, who was with her, and he ate it, too.

She wanted the wisdom it would give her; God had provided both she and Adam with everything they needed, what more did Eve think she needed when she had God Himself visiting her and Adam every day. When you do not totally trust God, the enemy will have you thinking God is trying to keep something from you. Scripture tells us in the greatest voice of counsel was in the midst of Eve every day, yet she chose to listen to the voice of Satan. Yes, today we need wisdom, in the garden all was needed was obedience to God. Now that sin has now entered in. We now have to choose daily between doing what's right over that which is wrong, we are under spiritual attack every day. The attacks come in various forms, we need the wisdom of God to help us make the right choices every day, no decision is too great or too small. Thank goodness God still graces His children with His power in spite of men's stupidity, all we need is to ask for it!

Understanding

The Greek word for understanding is Parakoloutheō. It means to attain (to get) or to fully know. **Proverbs 4:7 (AMP)** *7 The beginning of Wisdom is: get Wisdom (skillful and godly Wisdom)! [For skillful and godly Wisdom is the principal thing.] And with all you have gotten, get understanding (discernment, comprehension, and interpretation).* Christian Evangelist Raye Comfort says this "He who has ears to hear let him hear, but ears to hear does not mean we have understanding." The Hebrew word for understanding is Bina, it originates from another Hebrew word; Bin, meaning one who is skillful and prudent.

My mother, when first given a cell phone around the age of seventy, had access not only to a phone she could use at home but one she could use away from home also. It allowed her to be more accessible when we needed to talk to her. Though she had been given something that would allow us to reach her at a moment's notice it was of no use to her without having a proper understanding of how it worked. The phone had to be turned on, her home phone did not, the phone needed to remain charged if she was to benefit from it, her home phone did not, her cell phone required her to have an understanding regarding its functioning ability that her home phone did not require. No matter what you possess, if you do not have the proper understanding of what you have been given and how it operates, it is still of no value to you. Understanding speaks to how to apply and use a thing.

How unfortunate it would be to have access to a valuable gift intended to enhance your life yet fail to capitalize on it by treating it as something inconsequential. My husband says this: "When one does not know the value of a thing you will sell it for cheap or give it a way for free. Understanding is a prized possession; it is not to be wasted or underutilized. It can be a game changer; it can shift things from bad to good, from difficult to easy, from losing to winning in life. So go ahead, as the saying goes "Get at it" get as much understanding as you can, the more you obtain, the more you'll want once you start exploring.

Understanding can make the difference between living a good life, to living a great life. I do not know about you, but I want the best life God has to offer me. I do not want to struggle unnecessarily in areas of my life for things I have the power to accomplish with God's help. Understanding eliminates the guessing game; it places me in a position to be successful in all areas of my life. Look at what Psalm 32:8-9 tells us.

Psalm 32:8-9 (AMP)
[8] I [the Lord] will instruct you and teach you in the way you should go; I will counsel you with My eye upon you.
[9] Be not like the horse or the mule, which lack understanding, which must have their mouths held firm with bit and bridle, or else they will not come with you.

Understanding in this passage comes from the Hebrew word *Bin*; it's meaning is the same as the Hebrew word Bina; meaning to have a level of discernment and to be able to deal wisely.

Here is where you need to be honest with yourself, sit still and reflect on how many situations have you mismanaged because you lacked clear understanding of the matter. How much did it cost you? I'm not speaking merely of money, but sleep, peace, your happiness. If you and I could do some things over we would have gotten more clarity on the matter than forging ahead in our own ignorance, because that is what we are doing when we operate out of the scope of Godly understanding.

Proverbs 16:20-22 (KJV)
[20] He that handleth a matter wisely shall find good: and whoso trusteth in the LORD, happy is he.
[21] The wise in heart shall be called prudent: and the sweetness of the lips increaseth learning.

²² Understanding is a wellspring of life unto him that hath it: but the instruction of fools is folly.

There are never any mishaps, regrets, restless nights, or sadness when we manage matters wisely, only good. You are at peace even when God does not allow a situation to work out because you trust God knows what He is doing better than you, and that He would withhold no good thing from you when your way of life is aligned to His ways. That word good in the Hebrew is "Tob," English words used to describe Tob is best, merry, favor, prosperity. I know I'm not the only one who needs all of these things in their life. Yes, life comes with challenges and struggles but why go through unnecessary ones when you do not have to. In John 4 Jesus meets a Samaritan woman at the well who life was in shambles.

John 4:7-29 (NLT2)
⁷ Soon a Samaritan woman came to draw water, and Jesus said to her, "Please give me a drink."

⁸ He was alone at the time because his disciples had gone into the village to buy some food.

⁹ The woman was surprised, for Jews refuse to have anything to do with Samaritans. She said to Jesus, "You are a Jew, and I am a Samaritan woman. Why are you asking me for a drink?"

¹⁰ Jesus replied, "If you only knew the gift God has for you and who you are speaking to, you would ask me, and I would give you living water."

¹¹ "But sir, you don't have a rope or a bucket," she said, "and this well is very deep. Where would you get this living water?

¹² And besides, do you think you're greater than our ancestor Jacob, who gave us this well? How can you offer better water than he and his sons and his animals enjoyed?"

¹³ Jesus replied, "Anyone who drinks this water will soon become thirsty again.

¹⁴ *But those who drink the water I give will never be thirsty again. It becomes a fresh, bubbling spring within them, giving them eternal life."*

¹⁵ *"Please, sir," the woman said, "give me this water! Then I'll never be thirsty again, and I won't have to come here to get water."*

¹⁶ *"Go and get your husband," Jesus told her.*

¹⁷ *"I don't have a husband," the woman replied. Jesus said, "You're right! You don't have a husband—*

¹⁸ *for you have had five husbands, and you aren't even married to the man you're living with now. You certainly spoke the truth!"*

¹⁹ *"Sir," the woman said, "you must be a prophet.*

²⁰ *So tell me, why is it that you Jews insist that Jerusalem is the only place of worship, while we Samaritans claim it is here at Mount Gerizim, where our ancestors worshiped?"*

²¹ *Jesus replied, "Believe me, dear woman, the time is coming when it will no longer matter whether you worship the Father on this mountain or in Jerusalem.*

²² *You Samaritans know very little about the one you worship, while we Jews know all about him, for salvation comes through the Jews.*

²³ *But the time is coming—indeed it's here now—when true worshipers will worship the Father in spirit and in truth. The Father is looking for those who will worship him that way.*

²⁴ *For God is Spirit, so those who worship him must worship in spirit and in truth."*

²⁵ *The woman said, "I know the Messiah is coming—the one who is called Christ. When he comes, he will explain everything to us."*

²⁶ *Then Jesus told her, "I AM the Messiah!"*

²⁷ *Just then his disciples came back. They were shocked to find him talking to a woman, but none of them had the nerve to ask, "What do you want with her?" or "Why are you talking to her?"*

²⁸ *The woman left her water jar beside the well and ran back to the village, telling everyone,*

²⁹ *"Come and see a man who told me everything I ever did! Could he possibly be the Messiah?"*

Several things happened in the life of the Samaritan woman.

1. **The woman did not clearly understand who she was speaking with. John 4:10 (KJV)** ¹⁰ Jesus answered and said unto her, "If thou knewest the gift of God, and who it is that saith to thee, give me to drink; thou wouldest have asked of him, and he would have given thee living water." She supposed Him to be a prophet but did not know Him to be the Son of God that saves and delivers. Only God can give discernment/revelation to what you do not know.

2. **The Samaritan woman at the well had no idea nor understanding that she was living beneath God standards for her life.** she had no idea of who she really was, but once she met Jesus, she left converted. When someone can tell you everything about your life you have ever done, and leave their presence changed, wanting no more of your past sinful nature know, they were God sent.

3. **She went and shared her revelation with others. John 4:28-29 (KJV)** ²⁸ The woman then left her waterpot, and went her way into the city, and saith to the men, ²⁹ Come, see a man, which told me all things that ever I did: is not this the Christ? She received a word of knowledge and understanding about herself and who was speaking into her life. This kind of power can only come from God and those He chooses who are yielded to God to work through them.

Discretion

Discretion: To give attention to and behave wisely.

Daniel 2:12-13 (KJV)
^{12} For this cause the king was angry and very furious, and commanded to destroy all the wise men of Babylon.
^{13} And the decree went forth that the wise men should be slain; and they sought Daniel and his fellows to be slain.

King Nebuchadnezzar is upset that his astrologers cannot interpret his dream and has ordered all the wise men to be killed which included Daniel and the 3 Hebrew boys, whose name have been changed to Hananiah, Mishael, and Azariah.

In this story Daniel was able to interpret King Nebuchadnezzar's dream, and all ended up well for everyone involved. Why? From the onset Daniel operated with wisdom and discretion. *"When Arioch, the commander of the king's guard, came to kill them Daniel handled the situation with wisdom and discretion. Daniel 2:14 (NLT).* As stated earlier, when wisdom is utilized, your circumstances become a game changer. Daniel did not panic. I always say trouble will reveal who you really are and how you operate. Daniel did not rush into action. Daniel is an excellent example of acquiescing control of the situation and allowing God to take control. God drives much better than you and me, let Him take the wheel, He's guaranteed to keep you out of harm's way. He will even set you in positions you never even imagined!

Daniel 2:46-49 (KJV)
^{46} Then the king Nebuchadnezzar fell upon his face, and worshipped Daniel, and commanded that they should offer an oblation and sweet odours unto him.

⁴⁷ The king answered unto Daniel, and said, Of a truth it is, that your God is a God of gods, and a Lord of kings, and a revealer of secrets, seeing thou couldest reveal this secret.

⁴⁸ Then the king made Daniel a great man, and gave him many great gifts, and made him ruler over the whole province of Babylon, and chief of the governors over all the wise men of Babylon.

⁴⁹ Then Daniel requested of the king, and he set Shadrach, Meshach, and Abednego, over the affairs of the province of Babylon: but Daniel sat in the gate of the king.

I will discuss more on Daniel in a later chapter.

Proverbs 2:11 (HCSB)
¹¹ Discretion will watch over you, and understanding will guard you. Discretion will keep when you follow its guidance!

Counsel: The counsel that comes from Wisdom is the counsel of God! Isaiah 11:2 (KJV) ² And the spirit of the LORD shall rest upon him, the spirit of wisdom and understanding, the spirit of counsel and might, the spirit of knowledge and of the fear of the LORD.

Jesus Himself did not operate independently of the Spirit. He operated under the guidance of the Spirit's counsel. If Jesus Himself lived His life under the guidance of spiritual counsel, why wouldn't you and me? Jesus was consistently influenced by and relied upon every attribute of the Spirit. Remember Isaiah 11:2 does not speak of different Spirits; there is one Spirit but multiple characteristics of the Spirit. You and I have various characteristics, but they all come from the same person.

Jesus did not depend on His person but the one person that influenced everything He did: The Spirit. One of the Hebrew words for counsel is *Esa,* three English words used to define Esa is advice, (counsel) advisement, (scrutiny/analyze) and purpose (objection). When you and I rely on the counsel of Wisdom please take into consideration the counsel The Spirit of Wisdom gives is unmatched, The Spirit of Wisdom has taken all matters into consideration concerning your situation and has an ultimate purpose for the counsel it gives. Accept it to ensure things turns according to God's plans and not your own. We can only benefit from the counsel of Wisdom when we accept the counsel of Wisdom!

Reproof:

Reproof: Reproof by some is often thought of as negative communication. Some folks would rather do without it than be corrected. Agree with it or not, correction is beneficial for our lives; we all need it at times. Correction makes you and I better. A few years back I preached a message entitled "This May Hurt Now But There's A Reason For This" The message centered on the necessity of discipline! Regardless of whether it's a tough word of reproof or a punishment, there are those who scuff at being reprimanded, but scripture tells us this; "Open rebukes is better than love that is hidden," Proverbs 27:5 (AMP).

People who say they love you but won't correct you do not love you as much as they say they do. God loves you and I so much that He has to correct us. If God allowed us to go unchecked and live unrestrained lives having no accountability, living by our own standards; trust me the results would be disastrous. The Prodigal son soon realized he was much better off under the governing authority of His father, so He returned home, see Luke 15. The purpose of reproofing is to correct unruly behavior. It is the love of God that corrects us. Think of God's reproof this way; God doesn't stop loving us when He corrects us, He corrects us because He loves us!

Proverbs 3:11-12 (MSG)
[11] But don't, dear friend, resent GOD's discipline; don't sulk under his loving correction.

¹² It's the child he loves that GOD corrects; a father's delight is behind all this.

Each of these pillars is necessary for our continued development. I'm certain there are other valuable benefits we gain from following the guidance of Wisdom. These are merely the ones I chose to focus my attention on. Do not despise but rather embrace what God uses to cultivate your life. Father knows what's required and what's beneficial to help each of us reach our maximum potential in life.

Chapter Six
The Danger in Ignoring Wisdom's Voice

To reject any source of help God gives you is just plain dumb if you ask me, especially if you say, God, I trust you with my life. Please do not get offended; I'm not calling you dumb, but your decision to refuse assistance that is meant to better your quality of life is dumb. I once knew a person who refused the advice of their doctor that would have saved their life. It wasn't long after the person died. Because of their refusal to listen to the person who knew more about their medical condition than they did it cost the individual their life. Spiritual wisdom is just as vital to your life as the doctor's voice was to the life of the person I spoke of. You and I do not have to put our lives at risk or make repeated mistakes by living under the guidance of our own intelligence when God had given us spiritual intelligence that supersedes ours. The people in Proverbs ignored what was meant to be blessing in their lives.

Proverbs 1:24-33 (NLT2)

²⁴ "I called you so often, but you wouldn't come. I reached out to you, but you paid no attention.

²⁵ You ignored my advice and rejected the correction I offered.

²⁶ So I will laugh when you are in trouble! I will mock you when disaster overtakes you—

²⁷ when calamity overtakes you like a storm, when disaster engulfs you like a cyclone, and anguish and distress overwhelm you.

²⁸ "When they cry for help, I will not answer. Though they anxiously search for me, they will not find me.

²⁹ For they hated knowledge and chose not to fear the LORD.

³⁰ They rejected my advice and paid no attention when I corrected them.

³¹ Therefore, they must eat the bitter fruit of living their own way, choking on their own schemes.

³² For simpletons turn away from me—to Wisdom death. Fools are destroyed by their own complacency.

³³ But all who listen to me will live in peace, untroubled by fear of harm.

The verses in Proverbs chapter one speak to the danger in ignoring wisdoms voice. Proverbs 1:24 tell us that Wisdom called out to the people in this text not one time, but repeatedly! I'd be willing to bet it was not even three times, but well over that mark. If you grew up in the era of parenting when I was a child, you knew the danger of ignoring your parents' voices. There were always consequences when you did. If you are honest, your parents did and Wisdom did, speak to you repeatedly but you refused to respond. We should not think any different when it comes to adhering to the voice of God in our lives. There is always a penalty when you go outside the will of God and choose to do things your way.

I Samuel 8 tells us of a people who thought they knew better than God, they chose a plan for their lives that excluded God. "Do everything they say to you," the LORD replied, "for it is me they are rejecting, not you. They don't want me to be their king any longer. 1 Samuel 8:7 (NLT2). The people put their own desires above the desires of God and that will always lead to heartache. They could have saved themselves a lot of heartache and pain had they yielded to the will of God and not their own. I cannot think of a time any time in my life that I went against the will of God and it worked out well. Even if it started out looking like a blessing it ended in disaster.

1 Samuel 8:1-8 (NLT2)

[1] *As Samuel grew old, he appointed his sons to be judges over Israel.*

[2] *Joel and Abijah, his oldest sons, held court in Beersheba.*

[3] *But they were not like their father, for they were greedy for money. They accepted bribes and perverted justice.*

[4] *Finally, all the elders of Israel met at Ramah to discuss the matter with Samuel.*

[5] *"Look," they told him, "you are now old, and your sons are not like you. Give us a king to judge us like all the other nations have."*

[6] *Samuel was displeased with their request and went to the LORD for guidance.*

[7] *"Do everything they say to you," the LORD replied, "for it is me they are rejecting, not you. They don't want me to be their king any longer.*

[8] *Ever since I brought them from Egypt, they have continually abandoned me and followed other gods. And now they are giving you the same treatment.*

Samuel on the other hand understood the importance of living one's life under the influence and guidance of God. As I stated in proverbs 1:24 Wisdom called out to the people, but they didn't come, they rejected her voice instead. The children of Israel rejected God's voice. Even after Samuel warned them of the cruelty, they would experience under the king they chose. They said "No we shall have a king. 1 Samuel 8:19. ***The things you want for your life will never be better than the things of God.*** 1 Samuel 8:11- 17 tell us what the people chose as an alternative to what God wanted for them.

1 Samuel 8:11-17 (KJV)

^{11} And he said, This will be the manner of the king that shall reign over you: He will take your sons, and appoint them for himself, for his chariots, and to be his horsemen; and some shall run before his chariots.

^{12} And he will appoint him captains over thousands, and captains over fifties; and will set them to ear his ground, and to reap his harvest, and to make his instruments of war, and instruments of his chariots.

^{13} And he will take your daughters to be confectionaries, and to be cooks, and to be bakers.

^{14} And he will take your fields, and your vineyards, and your oliveyards, even the best of them, and give them to his servants.

^{15} And he will take the tenth of your seed, and of your vineyards, and give to his officers, and to his servants.

^{16} And he will take your menservants, and your maidservants, and your goodliest young men, and your asses, and put them to his work.

^{17} He will take the tenth of your sheep: and ye shall be his servants.

Saul would not have the people's best interest at heart; Everything would be about him and his desires, and yet they chose Saul to be their king. I do not know about you, but I would not want to serve under the leadership of anyone who thinks only of themselves. Everything God does is in the best interest of His children. Even when we mess up God does not give us the just punishment we truly deserve. God's Grace gives us what we do not deserve, and God's mercy keeps us from getting what we do deserve. God loves you and I just that much. He put His children's wellbeing above that of His own son. Who wouldn't serve a God like that? I'd say someone who does not truly know God. If you are a parent reading this book you can attest to the fact that there were times you held back a just due punishment for your child. Then there were times you had to turn a deaf ear in order for them to learn the lesson from their unruly behavior.

1 Samuel 8 19 tells us this "And in that day you will cry out because of your king, whom you have chosen for yourselves, but the Lord will not answer you in that day. As a youth whenever I or one my siblings found ourselves crying about a decision that turned out horribly wrong that our parents had prewarned us about, they would say this "You Made Your Bed Now You Will Have To lie In It." What they were saying was these are the consequences of our own choices; we may as well stop crying! We did not heed their warnings, and they are not interested in listening to our whining. There are times when we have to allow our children to go through the suffering of their own bad decisions making in hopes that they will learn the lessons intended. Not to hurt them but to help them.

The children of Israel had to learn the hard way because they trusted their own insight over God's! **Proverbs 28:26 (NLT2)** *²⁶ Those who trust their own insight are foolish, but anyone who walks in wisdom is safe.* How much better off our lives will be when we live our lives on the knowledge of God's insight than our own. In Apostle Paul's writings to The Corinthian Church, he says this, *"We Have Depended On God's Grace, Not On Our Own Human Wisdom, that Is How We Have Conducted Ourselves Before The World."* **2 Corinthians 1:12.** Things will always work out the way they are supposed to when you are God led, even when facing adversity.

There is a steep price you and I pay when we reject the help that is meant to safeguard us. I once heard Lady Jasmine Robinson say this, "When the Plan of God Is in Motion It Quiets The Commotion" Nothing is more calming and satisfying than living a God ordered life. When I say ordered, I mean a life that operates under His counsel and guidance. When I say commotion, I'm not speaking of disturbances and turmoil's that come when you are following God, those will come simply because you've chosen to follow God. I'm talking about the commotion that goes on in your head. In John 16:33 Jesus tells the disciples this, **"These things I have spoken unto you, that in me ye might have peace. In the world ye shall have tribulation: but be of good cheer; I have overcome the world.** There is a peace that comes when you trust God in spite of attacks. When you know you are in the will of God, you press on regardless of regardless of who or what tries to stop you. When the armies of the Moabites, Ammonites, and some of the Meunites declared war on Jehoshaphat, Jehoshaphat sought the insight of God. Below is Jehoshaphat's prayer.

2 Chronicles 20:5-12 (NLT2)
⁵ Jehoshaphat stood before the community of Judah and Jerusalem in front of the new courtyard at the Temple of the LORD.

⁶ He prayed, "O LORD, God of our ancestors, you alone are the God who is in heaven. You are ruler of all the kingdoms of the earth. You are powerful and mighty; no one can stand against you!

⁷ O our God, did you not drive out those who lived in this land when your people Israel arrived? And did you not give this land forever to the descendants of your friend Abraham?

⁸ Your people settled here and built this Temple to honor your name.

⁹ They said, 'Whenever we are faced with any calamity such as war, plague, or famine, we can come to stand in your presence before this Temple where your name is honored. We can cry out to you to save us, and you will hear us and rescue us.'

¹⁰ "And now see what the armies of Ammon, Moab, and Mount Seir are doing. You would not let our ancestors invade those nations when Israel left Egypt, so they went around them and did not destroy them.

¹¹ Now see how they reward us! For they have come to throw us out of your land, which you gave us as an inheritance.

¹² O our God, won't you stop them? We are powerless against this mighty army that is about to attack us. We do not know what to do, but we are looking to you for help."

Can I tell you help came; Jehoshaphat and his people did not even have to fight.

2 Chronicles 20:14-17 (NLT2)
¹⁴ the Spirit of the LORD came upon one of the men standing there. His name was Jahaziel son of Zechariah, son of Benaiah, son of Jeiel, son of Mattaniah, a Levite who was a descendant of Asaph.

¹⁵ He said, "Listen, all you people of Judah and Jerusalem! Listen, King Jehoshaphat! This is what the LORD says: Do not be afraid! Don't be discouraged by this mighty army, for the battle is not yours, but God's.

¹⁶ Tomorrow, march out against them. You will find them coming up through the ascent of Ziz at the end of the valley that opens into the wilderness of Jeruel.

¹⁷ But you will not even need to fight. Take your positions; then stand still and watch the LORD's victory. He is with you, O people of Judah and Jerusalem. Do not be afraid or discouraged. Go out against them tomorrow, for the LORD is with you!"

The enemies turned on themselves; when Jehoshaphat and his men arrived all they saw were dead bodies. They plundered the enemy and returned home.

2 Chronicles 20:29-30 (NLT2)
²⁹ When all the surrounding kingdoms heard that the LORD himself had fought against the enemies of Israel, the fear of God came over them.

³⁰ So Jehoshaphat's kingdom was at peace, for his God had given him rest on every side.

Some people can't experience this kind of peace because they have not learned to let God do the leading, they have not learned to seek God's voice on the matter. If you are reading this, aren't you tired of losing? Wouldn't you rather win? Let me insert this; success is not always things turning out the way you planned, but rather turning out the way, God planned. I'm certain Joseph would rather have never found himself in Egypt living with

Pharoah, however; scripture tells us, "*What Others Meant For Evil God Meant For Good To Save The Lives Of Many. "Gen 50:20.* The late Charles Stanley puts it this way "What appears to us as a valley of weeping is God's valley of preparation for godliness and service." When we find ourselves facing difficulties, we must trust that the All-knowing, All Wise God has a plan and will work things out according to His will and our good. Remember Jesus endured the unbearable pain of the cross that paid for the sins of humanity. When God is in it, know that His plans are perfect even during times, we may have to endure pain.

Next Proverbs 1:25 tells us the people rejected the correction Wisdom offered. I previously discussed reproof earlier in this chapter, to which you may refer if needed.

Proverbs 1:26-28 (NLT)
[26] So I will laugh when you are in trouble! I will mock you when disaster overtakes you—

[7] when calamity overtakes you like a storm, when disaster engulfs you like a cyclone, and anguish and distress overwhelm you.

[28] "When they cry for help, I will not answer. Though they anxiously search for me, they will not find me.

I don't know about you but, I'm sure there are instances where God laughed at some of my own dumb decision making. God will allow you to be dumb if you insist on being so. Please know God is not into making you and I do anything against our own will. The only person who will pay the price for your ignorance is you. That may sound harsh, but it's the truth. The reason behind this is because far too many of His children have the same mindset as the people did in **Proverbs 1:29-32** .*[29] For they hated knowledge and chose not to fear the LORD. [30] They rejected my advice and paid no attention when I corrected them. [31] Therefore, they must eat the bitter fruit of living their own way, choking on their own schemes.*

How often have God's children become upset with Him concerning situations they found themselves in when in fact the circumstances were as a result of their own actions, thereby attributing blame to God for the bitter consequences of their own decisions, having chosen their own path rather than God's purpose and plan for their lives. God will allow us to learn life lessons the hard way if that's the way we choose to learn. Life comes with enough difficulties of its own, I don't need to incur more problems by thinking I'm wiser than I actually am. The joy and blessing in listening to Wisdom's voice is found in Proverb 1:33. *³³* ***But all who listen to me will live in peace, untroubled by fear of evil.*** Even though we live in a world full of unrest (disturbances) we can still be at peace! So, don't be a simpleton. Human wisdom can never be trusted or considered concerning spiritual matters. Flesh can never be the lead influencer on where God wants to take you and when God seeks to use you! It is His way or the highway. If you know anything about a highway you understand a highway leads one down many paths; there is only one path that leads to the things of God, His. Human wisdom can never be relied upon for the believer who says they want to be led by God because His thought and ways are unlike ours.

Isaiah 55:8-9 (NLT2)
⁸ "My thoughts are nothing like your thoughts," says the LORD. "And my ways are far beyond anything you could imagine.

⁹ For just as the heavens are higher than the earth, so my ways are higher than your ways and my thoughts higher than your thoughts.

We must completely follow God's lead on anything He ask us to do. There are times when God makes a request that will not make sense to you and I. Few if any could have responded to God with the same level of devotion as Abraham did, when asked to offer Isaac up as a sacrifice. Scripture tells us Abraham got up early the next morning saddled his donkey and went on his way, no questions asked, (Gen 22). Thank goodness God isn't asking His children to make this kind of sacrifice today I question if any could. We'd have questions, not the child I've waited all these years to have, this cannot be God! You know I'm telling the truth. Remember this, God always has a greater blessing in store anytime you are willing to make the ultimate sacrifice. He sent the prophet Elijah to a woman who had only enough food for she and her son during a famine. A woman who had plans for she and her son to die, however God had greater plans. She fed Elijah first as the man of God requested and afterwards, she had food until the famine passed. (I Kings 17). Could you be preventing God from doing something greater in your life, because you have forgotten He does not operate like you!

Ask God to give you an ear to recognize His voice. Proverbs 8:4 tells us "Wisdom calls out to all people. There are a few reasons I can think of as to why we reject wisdom; **we do not like what we hear.** The sole purpose of Wisdom's voice is to offer the ear that listens something of value. Wisdom never speaks to do harm. But the wisdom from above is first of all pure (undefiled); then it is peace-loving, courteous (considerate, gentle). [It is willing to] yield to reason, full of compassion and good fruits; it is wholehearted *and* straightforward, impartial *and* unfeigned (free from doubts, wavering, and insincerity)**. James 3:17 (AMP)** Everything we read in this passage of scripture about wisdom is good.

The second reason, one in which I can sympathize with; **the person is unfamiliar with the wisdoms voice.** This can only be a short-term excuse. At some point you need to familiar yourself with the voice of Wisdom. Our children are able to respond to our voices even if other adult voices are around because they are familiar with them; they hear it on a daily basis. Wisdom's voice is God's voice; get to know the language of God and you will recognize when wisdom is speaking. Wisdom's voice aligns with God's Spirit and word. Familiarize yourself with both. **You Will Never Benefit From Anything You Constantly Ignore!**

Chapter Seven
Living Your Blessed Life

I often hear people say they are living their best life. This is commonly stated when things are going well in the individual's life and all things have aligned the way they hoped for. The person(s) is usually enjoying a life free from chaos, or displeasure of any kind. They are experiencing a level of happiness they've been waiting for. Sadly, happiness for this kind of individual is based upon happenings. The happy life Proverbs 13 speaks of is not built upon happenings; this happy life comes by way of righteous living. A blessed life will always be far better than a happy life because it does not factor in things always aligning to our comfort level but rather God's plans and purpose for our lives.

Proverbs 3:13-18 (AMP)
13 Happy (blessed, fortunate, enviable) is the man who finds skillful and godly Wisdom, and the man who gets understanding [drawing it forth from God's Word and life's experiences],
14 For the gaining of it is better than the gaining of silver, and the profit of it better than fine gold.
15 Skillful and godly Wisdom is more precious than rubies; and nothing you can wish for is to be compared to her.

¹⁶ Length of days is in her right hand, and in her left hand are riches and honor.

¹⁷ Her ways are highways of pleasantness, and all her paths are peace.

¹⁸ She is a tree of life to those who lay hold on her; and happy (blessed, fortunate, to be envied) is everyone who holds her fast.

When you read this passage of scripture out of Proverbs concerning Wisdom how can you not get excited about Wisdom being an essential dynamic in your life. Proverbs 3: 13 reads; *happy is the man who finds skillful and godly wisdom,* find here denotes more than just finding wisdom but one who acquires it, attains it; possess it. I believe I've made my point. You and I can find a thing, and it never adds any value to our lives. Why, because we merely found it. The believer must secure Wisdom. How do I secure Wisdom? You secure Wisdom by allowing wisdom to take residence in your life by yielding to its counsel. I can find the house of my dreams, but the house does not become mine simply because I found it. There is a process to securing the home of my dreams. Implementing the guidelines put in place to secure the home is what makes the home mine. It is only then that I can benefit from the shelter and contents its provides.

Far too often God's children spend too much time seeking to experience a happy life rather than a blessed life. The person who understands what it means to live a blessed life understands their life will not be exempt from trouble. Scripture tells us; "In the world ye shall have tribulation: but be of good cheer; I have overcome the world" (John 16:33). So, if your being happy is based upon everything going well on any given day, you will never experience a happy life in the manner in which God intended.

To discover something means it was always there. Since Wisdom has always been around let me share with you a few more reasons why the believer does benefit from wisdom. One being, His children do not feel the need to have Wisdom in their life; and secondly, His children think they are wiser, which means you have a huge amount of deception going on in your head. Which may suggest to some that you are stupid, but I'm not calling you stupid, I choose to call you unwise.

To discover something also implies one's ability to gain knowledge of a thing. Once Wisdom is welcomed and received it becomes yours and my responsibility to gain as much insight as we can. Wisdom speaks and instructs; but only to the one that is yielding. You cannot find Wisdom and your whole inner man is not fulfilled; no matter what life throws at you. Wisdom enables you to conqueror the difficulties of life. Wisdom understands how to manage the challenges of life. Wisdom understands all the money in the world is not enough to get you through heartache and pain. Money isn't enough when the doctor gives your loved one a death sentence. Though wealth can bring a sense of fulfillment, it fails in comparison to the fulfillment that comes with finding godly wisdom.

Proverbs 3:14-15
[14] For the gaining of it is better than the gaining of silver, and the profit of it better than fine gold. [15] Skillful and godly Wisdom is more precious than rubies; and nothing you can wish for is to be compared to her.

No amount of money can compare to the satisfaction one gets from having wisdom operating in their life. I'm certain we all know of or have heard about some miserable rich people. Rich people are constantly worrying about remaining rich. How many times have you turned on the news and read about a wealthy person who committed suicide? The first thing many people will ask is what made the person want to commit suicide with all the money they had. Yes, I know Ecclesiastes 10:19 says money answers all things, but let's look at the two verses before verse 19.

Ecclesiastes 10:17-19 (AMP)
> [17] *Happy (fortunate and to be envied) are you, O land, when your king is a free man and of noble birth and character and when your officials feast at the proper time—for strength and not for drunkenness!*
> [18] *Through indolence the rafters [of state affairs] decay and the roof sinks in, and through idleness of the hands the house leaks.*
> [19] *[Instead of repairing the breaches, the officials] make a feast for laughter, serve wine to cheer life, and [depend on tax] money to answer for all of it.*

There was an oversight in the state of affairs of the house by governing officials through idleness. Instead of repairing the building they were consumed with partying while depending on tax money to pay for all of it. The leaders were undisciplined and immature. Had wisdom been applied, these leaders would have demonstrated greater foresight and exercised responsible leadership, in line with the foundation of their God given responsibilities that prioritized what is right over their personal indulgence. If money answered all issues, there would be no need for God in our lives.

While money can provide comfort, beautiful things, and great vacations, what it cannot do is inform you and me on what we were created for and how we are to live out our lives. I do not know about you but give me God every day of the week!

Psalm 49:6-8 (KJV)

[6] *They that trust in their wealth, and boast themselves in the multitude of their riches;*

[7] *None of them can by any means redeem his brother, nor give to God a ransom for him:*

[8] *(For the redemption of their soul is precious, and it ceaseth for ever:)* Right here you can see money does not answer everything. We must always make certain we never take scripture out of context!

Money may provide you with a lavish life, but it cannot provide you with a blessed life and eternal life!

If your source of happiness depends solely on money, you are in for a rude awakening. There will come a day when you realize there are certain things money can't buy, like peace, joy, fulfillment in life, or what "The Temptations" call a cloud nine level of happiness or bliss. According to "The Temptations" in order to experience a cloud nine level of happiness you have to take cloud nine, leaving all your troubles behind. Listen to the lyrics of this popular song recorded by "The Temptations."

(Cloud Nine) You can be what you wanna be
(Cloud Nine) You ain't got no responsibility
(Cloud Nine) Every man, every man is free
(Cloud Nine) You're a million miles from reality (Reality)

I'm gonna sail up, up, higher, up, up
Up, up and away
Cloud Nine

I wanna say I love the life I live
And I'm gonna live the life I love
Up here on Cloud Nine
I'm riding high on Cloud Nine

You're as free as a bird in flight
(Cloud Nine) There's no difference between day and night
(Cloud Nine) It's a world of love and harmony
(Cloud Nine) You're a million miles from reality (Reality)

News flash this is not reality! Wisdom will teach you how to live and deal with life's challenges, not run from them. I choose to live in a Holy blissful state instead; one where my circumstances do not dictate my level of happiness. One where I can love the life I live even when things are not going the way I want at the moment. I can be Happy because someone greater is dictating the direction of my life even when things are not perfect.

Proverbs 3:16 (AMP)
^{16} Length of days is in her right hand, and in her left hand are riches and honor.

I do not know about you, but I want to live out as many days on earth as I can. God assured us of at least 3 score and ten, I want to live that many and beyond; I hope you do as well. We've all heard the phrase they died too soon. This is usually stated when an individual dies at an early age. Perhaps like me you have known someone who died young, not because of a sickness, but due to the kind of life they lived carelessly. They lived a life of drugs, alcoholism, gangs and violent crimes. Things that could have been avoided had Wisdom been applied. Yes, God knows when each of us will die, but God is not responsible for how we die. Sometimes men die at the hands of their own doing, by living and doing things outside the will and Wisdom of God. For the one who embraces Wisdom's guidance, Wisdom will add days to their life, not take from it. Yes, there are people who live long lives; but my question is this, is the quality of the long life they have lived worth living a long life? I want both longevity and quality of life.

Scripture tells us in Jeremiah 29:11 (NLT2)
^{11} For I know the plans I have for you," says the LORD. "They are plans for good and not for disaster, to give you a future and a hope.

Sinful plans that do not include God and do not line up with the word of God inevitably yield disastrous outcomes. Christ came that we might have and enjoy life in abundance. (John 10:10) God never meant for His children to live their lives any kind of way, He has a standard and rules for His children to live by. If your standard for living the blessed life does not include the rules and mandates of God, you are living beneath God's standard's; I do not care how much money and pleasure you may be experiencing.

Proverbs 21:21 (KJV)
^{21} He that followeth after righteousness and mercy findeth life, righteousness, and honour. Right living encompasses life, righteousness and honour! We have no clue as to how to live right without the guidance of Wisdom, so if you are out here going it on your own stop it!

Proverbs 3:17-18
^{17} Her ways are highways of pleasantness, and all her paths are peace.
^{18} She is a tree of life to those who lay hold on her; and happy (blessed, fortunate, to be envied) is everyone who holds her fast.

Look at the road Wisdom leads you down, pleasantness and peace. Unfortunately, life will throw you unexpected curves, steeps and slopes; and rough paths, so we should want to experience as much peace in life as we can. Wisdom enables us to experience pleasantness and peace with these ever-changing conditions. Occasionally during a flight, you may encounter turbulence; however, the route to your destination is what it is. The Pilot is unlikely to change course if he is too far into the flight. What he does is notify the passenger of the turbulence and advises them he is going to try and find smoother airspace. What the pilot will do is ascend to a higher altitude than the current flight level until they reach less turbulent airspace.

Allow wisdom to pilot your life before and during turbulence. Wisdom equips you with solutions that make the situation less stressful on you, not necessarily remove it. What wisdom does is remove the weight and power of its ability to rob you of your peace and joy. So, take hold of Wisdom and never make a move without it. Do as Proverbs 4:13 KJV says, [13] Take fast hold of instruction; let her not go: keep her; for she is thy life. Wisdom is a conduit of life, it makes life more enjoyable through the good and the bad, never forget that! The blessed life is a life under the influence and guidance of Wisdom.

Chapter Eight
The Courage & Faithfulness of Wisdom

I don't know about you, but I wholeheartedly believe it requires a tremendous amount of faith and courage to maintain your stance on a matter when the consequences of non-compliance of what you have been the instructions to do is death. Few people have the courage to look an imposed death sentence in the face and say let the chips fall where they may. Few people are willing to put their life on the line all for the cause of living life God's way. Few feel it is even necessary to have to make this kind of sacrifice on behalf of God. There are three men in the Bible who were willing to do just that. Their names are Daniel, Hananiah, Mishael, Azariah whose names were changed by Nebuchadnezzar's chief of staff to Belteshazzar, Shadrach, Meshach and Abednego. These men demonstrated great courage and faith during one of the most challenging times in their lives. They visibly demonstrated the wisdom through the Respect, Reverence and Reliance they had in God. They were loyal, putting nothing and no one above God.

Daniel was the leader of these men. One thing every believer need in their life is someone to lead them in the things of God. It was Daniel who from the onset was determined not to defile himself by eating the food and wine given to them by the King. ***Daniel 1:8 (NLT2)*** *⁸ But Daniel was determined not to defile himself by eating the food and wine given to them by the king. He asked the chief of staff for permission not to eat these unacceptable foods.* You have to have a mindset that says I will not accept everything the world offers me. As stated earlier, the worlds systems are flawed, in many cases downright corrupt; therefore, cannot be relied upon. Daniel's and the three Hebrew boys first test were to reject the king's food. In doing so they looked more nourished and healthier than the men who had eaten the Kings food. You will always be better off rejecting what the world offers you. It may look good, taste good, or even make you feel good. Never compromise your spiritual values for worldly gratification. The world will offer you lots of money, shiny big toys, but reject it; why, because there is always a price to pay for the things the world offers you. They are short-term effects that will soon wear off, eventually leaving you in a miserable state. God riches are eternal; God takes care of the child who put their trust and confidence in Him.

Psalm 146:3-8 (NLT2)
³ Don't put your confidence in powerful people; there is no help for you there.
⁴ When they breathe their last, they return to the earth, and all their plans die with them.
⁵ But joyful are those who have the God of Israel as their helper, whose hope is in the LORD their God.
⁶ He made heaven and earth, the sea, and everything in them. He keeps every promise forever.
⁷ He gives justice to the oppressed and food to the hungry. The LORD frees the prisoners.

⁸ The LORD opens the eyes of the blind. The LORD lifts up those who are weighed down. The LORD loves the godly.

When these four men training was over and they went before the king to talk, no one impressed the king more than they.

Daniel 1:19-20 (NLT2)
¹⁹ The king talked with them, and no one impressed him as much as Daniel, Hananiah, Mishael, and Azariah. So, they entered the royal service.
²⁰ Whenever the king consulted them in any matter requiring wisdom and balanced judgment, he found them ten times more capable than any of the magicians and enchanters in his entire kingdom.

Why do you suppose these young men were so wise? Because these men walked and talked with God. Later the king has a dream he could not understand, and his astrologers could not help him, so the king threatened to kill everyone even Daniel and his friend. Daniel, however, managed the manner with wisdom.

Daniel 2:14 (NLT2)
¹⁴ When Arioch, the commander of the king's guard, came to kill them, Daniel handled the situation with wisdom and discretion.

Daniel 2:16-18 (NLT2)
¹⁶ Daniel went at once to see the king and requested more time to tell the king what the dream meant.
¹⁷ Then Daniel went home and told his friends Hananiah, Mishael, and Azariah what had happened.
¹⁸ He urged them to ask the God of heaven to show them his mercy by telling them the secret, so they would not be executed along with the other wise men of Babylon.

You do not pray to a God you have no connection with. To make a long story short, the secret was revealed to Daniel, so he, his friends and the astrologers' lives were spared. May we all be blessed to have friends like Daniel, friends who are aligned to God and know how to seek the face of God in your crisis especially if they are a part of it. After Daniel revealed the meaning of the Kings dream, something interesting happens:

Daniel 2:46-47 (NLT2)
⁴⁶ Then King Nebuchadnezzar threw himself down before Daniel and worshiped him, and he commanded his people to offer sacrifices and burn sweet incense before him.

⁴⁷ The king said to Daniel, "Truly, your God is the greatest of gods, the LORD over kings, a revealer of mysteries, for you have been able to reveal this secret."

Now before you get upset over the Kings worship of Daniels, know that Daniel did not accept worship that belongs to God. Listen to the kings' words; "Truly your God is the greatest of gods, the Lord is over kings, a revealer of mysteries." The King was in fact stating to Daniel, God's greatness and the fact that the Lord is over all kings, he said nothing of Daniels greatness and him being Lord over kings, he acknowledged everything spoken to him by Daniel was revealed to Daniel by God. Though the king spared Daniel, his friends and the life of the wise men he could not be trusted. Here lies the problem with worldly systems, and why they cannot be relied upon. Simply acknowledging a deity does not necessarily mean the person accepts that deity as their own God. The same king would later make a golden statue in which he would worship and mandated everyone else to worship.

Daniel 3:1 (NLT2)
¹ King Nebuchadnezzar made a gold statue ninety feet tall and nine feet wide and set it up on the plain of Dura in the province of Babylon.

Daniel 3:5-6 (NLT2)
⁵ When you hear the sound of the horn, flute, zither, lyre, harp, pipes, and other musical instruments, bow to the ground to worship King Nebuchadnezzar's gold statue.

⁶ Anyone who refuses to obey will immediately be thrown into a blazing furnace."

The three Hebrew boys refused, to obey the order. Read the entire story for yourself in Daniel chapter 3. I'm just giving you a summary of their story. Look at the bold statement these men made to the king.

Daniel 3:16-19 (NLT2)
¹⁶ Shadrach, Meshach, and Abednego replied, "O Nebuchadnezzar, we do not need to defend ourselves before you.

¹⁷ If we are thrown into the blazing furnace, the God whom we serve is able to save us. He will rescue us from your power, Your Majesty.

¹⁸ But even if he doesn't, we want to make it clear to you, Your Majesty, that we will never serve your gods or worship the gold statue you have set up."

¹⁹ Nebuchadnezzar was so furious with Shadrach, Meshach, and Abednego that his face became distorted with rage. He commanded that the furnace be heated seven times hotter than usual.

You are never to justify your relationship with God by conforming to the rules and mandates of a worldly system. You justify it by remaining aligned with God and His mandates; when you do, God will justify you. Consider this: if God does not fulfil your request will you remain steadfast in your faith. If He does not respond within your expected time period, will you persist in your devotion to Him or will you seek alternatives solutions to your problem. We must be all in with God at all times. The men were indeed thrown in the fire however they did not die because God stood in the fire with them. ²⁵ "Look!" Nebuchadnezzar shouted. "I see four men, unbound, walking around in the fire unharmed! And the fourth looks like a god!" Daniel 3:25 (NLT) When the men came out of the fire pay attention to the words of King Nebuchadnezzar.

Daniel 3:28-29 (NLT2)
²⁸ Then Nebuchadnezzar said, "Praise to the God of Shadrach, Meshach, and Abednego! He sent his angel to rescue his servants who trusted in him. They defied the king's command and were willing to die rather than serve or worship any god except their own God.

²⁹ Therefore, I make this decree: If any people, whatever their race or nation or language, speak a word against the God of Shadrach, Meshach, and Abednego, they will be torn limb from limb, and their houses will be turned into heaps of rubble. There is no other god who can rescue like this!"

God will vindicate you and your adversaries will be forced to change their stance. There are persons who have stated to my husband they have warned individuals to refrain from speaking negatively about him stating God protects him. Things did not turn out well for them. Their downfall was not a result of my husband's retaliation, but rather a consequence of him operating in wisdom concerning them. While it is natural to want to retaliate when wronged, it requires divine wisdom to resist impulse and instead seek guidance through prayer, allowing oneself to hear God's voice and direction. Get out of attack mode and get into prayer mode so you can hear the voice of God.

Daniels Test

The Hits keep Coming!

Daniel 6:1-10 (NLT2)

¹ Darius the Mede decided to divide the kingdom into 120 provinces, and he appointed a high officer to rule over each province.

² The king also chose Daniel and two others as administrators to supervise the high officers and protect the king's interests.

³ Daniel soon proved himself more capable than all the other administrators and high officers. Because of Daniel's great ability, the king made plans to place him over the entire empire.

⁴ Then the other administrators and high officers began searching for some fault in the way Daniel was handling government affairs, but they couldn't find anything to criticize or condemn. He was faithful, always responsible, and completely trustworthy.

⁵ So they concluded, "Our only chance of finding grounds for accusing Daniel will be in connection with the rules of his religion."

⁶ So the administrators and high officers went to the king and said, "Long live King Darius!

⁷ We are all in agreement—we administrators, officials, high officers, advisers, and governors—that the king should make a law that will be strictly enforced. Give orders that for the next thirty days any person who prays to anyone, divine or human—except to you, Your Majesty—will be thrown into the den of lions.

⁸ And now, Your Majesty, issue and sign this law so it cannot be changed, an official law of the Medes and Persians that cannot be revoked."

⁹ So King Darius signed the law.

¹⁰ But when Daniel learned that the law had been signed, he went home and knelt down as usual in his upstairs room, with its windows open toward Jerusalem. He prayed three times a day, just as he had always done, giving thanks to his God.

I love the chronicles of Daniel and his friends because it shows that as believer's we can withstand the opposing forces of the enemy without compromising or betraying our Godly values! Too many times, as born again, blood bought citizens of the Kingdom of God who have been given authority and power to overcome all forms of adversity we turn a blind eye. We bow down, give in, run away from and quit on God. There are several reasons for this, we have forgotten who we are, we do not believe who we are, we fear the enemy more than we trust God, or we try to please the enemy and God. You cannot serve two masters Mathew 6:24 (KJV). Only one can be your Lord, only one can govern your way of life. These men did not do that, they took a stand, a strong stand against the enemy! These men were proof that just because you are under bondage does not mean you have let it to govern your actions. Something my husband shared with our congregation, **"Your Enemies Wants To Force You Into A Place Of Fear, So They Don't Have To Deal With You In Your Place And Stance Of Faith In God."** Some of you need to tell the enemy, deal with it. The moment they mess with God's children; they have invited God to the fight.

I don't care who you are serving under whether by force or your own free choice, if you say you are a believer and the person you are serving under demands you to go against the principles and teaching of God; you should and must take a stand. You are either for the Lord, or you are not, that includes false prophets also and trust me there are plenty of them. Matthew 12:30 (NLT2) "Anyone who isn't with me opposes me, and anyone who isn't collaborating with me is actually working against me when it comes to the things of God. There is no middle ground! You're either working on behalf of the Kingdom or you're not! You're standing with God or you're not! Either you believe God, or you do not!

I John 4:4 (NLT2)
⁴ But you belong to God, my dear children. You have already won a victory over those people because the Spirit who lives in you is greater than the spirit who lives in the world.

John 4:4 mentions two key things; **you belong to God** and **you have already won the victory!** So, when the challenge comes no matter what it is, you need to remind yourself; you are God's child and He is with you in the fight, and you have already won! You should never go to battle with a mindset that states I may not win. Do not be like the children of Israel who went into their promise land, came back with the goods and then talked themselves out of what God said was theirs. Thank goodness Joshua and Caleb hand a different mindset that said, "The Lord Is With Us Do Not Fear."

Stop giving your enemy power and control over you that he does not really have! Daniel understood this. The King may have imprisoned Daniel physically, but Daniel was not imprisoned mentally or spiritually! Daniel lived in King Darius Kingdom, but he was not of his kingdom. Philippians 3:20. But we are citizens of heaven, where the Lord Jesus Christ lives. Our lives are governed by different laws. The worlds laws and mandates do not overrule what God has mandated for His children.

Wisdom will never lead you to do what is wrong, even in demanding situations. Wisdom always had your best interest at heart. Wisdom will instruct you on when to speak and when to keep silent, when to move and when to stay put.

When I was younger my friends and I really didn't know anything about the term stand your ground when we were put in a position of having to defend ourselves. What we would do is draw a line in the dirt! The line represented the person taking a stand; you cross this line, and the fight is on. One of the most crucial lessons you need to understand as a believer is to know your weapon of warfare! Some of you are not winning because you're fighting the wrong way and with the wrong weapon. You're trying to fight your enemy in the flesh when you should be fighting the enemy in the spirit realm! The enemy attacks you and you go straight to your flesh looking for a way to defeat them.

I was never so embarrassed of an illustration by the leadership of a women's organization I was a part of did to give the audience a picture of how you fight Satan. The enemy is on one side dressed in his battle gear and the individual who represented the Kingdom of God was in their battle gear! The Kingdom fighter had on her rob and boxing gloves and the enemy had on their robe and gloves, if I recall correctly, it was a red robe because you do know there is this crazy notion that Satan only wears red; maybe that's why so many believers are defeated from the start because they have been deceived from the start, they don't even recognize the enemy! Let me clue you in, Satan has influencers who wear pumps, skirts, pin stripped suits, robes, collars, and a variety of other outfits! It's not even about the outfit; it's about understanding the demonic spirit the person carries!

Back to the illustration I was sharing. The Kingdom believer starts fighting the enemy with those dumb boxing gloves she was wearing swinging and missing, I sat there in my chair with my head held down, saying Lord what are they doing! My spirit was screaming you're wearing the wrong armor and tell your trainer to pray. The believer's armor is found in Ephesians 6:10-13.

Ephesians 6:10-13 (KJV)
[10] Finally, my brethren, be strong in the Lord, and in the power of his might.
[11] Put on the whole armour of God, that ye may be able to stand against the wiles of the devil.
[12] For we wrestle not against flesh and blood, but against principalities, against powers, against the rulers of the darkness of this world, against spiritual wickedness in high places.
[13] Wherefore take unto you the whole armour of God, that ye may be able to withstand in the evil day, and having done all, to stand.

You cannot beat the enemy fighting in your flesh, this is spiritual warfare and it must be fought in the Spirit realm with spiritual weapons!

I wanted to get up and leave after that sad illustration of how Kingdom children should fight! **You and I must have a no compromise law:** The worldly systems have their laws that you cannot cross or there is a price to pay, so must we. If you start giving up one thing for your enemy, he will require you to eventually give up something else! **Stick to what you've always done; trust in who you have always relied upon, don't go changing now.** Do not revert back to old habits. Keep clinging to your confidence and trust in God.

But when Daniel learned that the law had been signed, he went home and knelt down as usual in his upstairs room, with its windows open toward Jerusalem. He prayed three times a day, just as he had always done, giving thanks to his God. **Daniel 6:10(NLT)**

The worst thing you can do is fall prey to the enemies' scare tactics. Once they know this is all it takes for you to betray God, they will use them on you for the rest of your life. They will bully you every chance they get! The only way to get a bully to stop tormenting you is to stand up against them. You've been trusting God all this time; now is not the time to back down; this is the time for you to stand front and center and show the enemy who you really are!

Daniel never sought King Darius for help. Daniel relied on what he's always relied on, his God. Too often His children make the mistake of seeking outside sources, God has a proven record and has always provides us with the help we need. If God chooses to use additional people or resources to help you, He can do that but seek Him first and let Him tell you firsthand. Do not assume your friend or parent has the answer to your situation, even if they have given you great advice in the past. Let God do the leading and the choosing. He may do things differently this time.

Daniel had been walking in Wisdom since he first stepped foot in the royal palace. **Daniel 1:17 (NLT2)** *¹⁷ God gave these four young men an unusual aptitude for understanding every aspect of literature and wisdom. And God gave Daniel the special ability to interpret the meanings of visions and dreams.*

Daniel was given an unusual aptitude for wisdom, a level of proficiency in the area of wisdom like none other. God always gives us the appropriate amount of what's needed for every circumstance we encounter in life. Daniel was equipped with all he needed from day one. You and I are never lacking the thing (s) needed to fulfill any God assignment. We are never without sufficient help to get us through every trial that comes our way. We must remember that God already knows every challenging moment we will face in life. God did not save His children and then wait until they get in trouble to empower them with the help they need, He empowered us the moment we excepted Christ into our hearts. The problem is at times we do not operate in the power He has already given us. The disciple had this same problem. **Matthew 10:1 (NLT2)** *¹ Jesus called his twelve disciples together and gave them authority to cast out evil spirits and to heal every kind of disease and illness.* They were given what they needed, however later in Mathew 17 they failed to operate in the power given to them.

Matthew 17:14-20 (NLT2)

¹⁴ At the foot of the mountain, a large crowd was waiting for them. A man came and knelt before Jesus and said,

¹⁵ "Lord, have mercy on my son. He has seizures and suffers terribly. He often falls into the fire or into the water.

¹⁶ So I brought him to your disciples, but they couldn't heal him."

¹⁷ Jesus replied, "You faithless and corrupt people! How long must I be with you? How long must I put up with you? Bring the boy to me."

¹⁸ Then Jesus rebuked the demon in the boy, and it left him. From that moment, the boy was well.

¹⁹ Afterward, the disciples asked Jesus privately, "Why couldn't we cast out that demon?"

²⁰ "You don't have enough faith," Jesus told them. "I tell you the truth, if you had faith even as small as a mustard seed, you could say to this mountain, 'Move from here to there,' and it would move. Nothing would be impossible."

This upset Christ because the disciples had it within them to set this demon-possessed boy free. You have it within you to overcome whatever it is life throws your way. It grieves God when His children walk around helpless, as if they were left on their own, powerless, unable to defend themselves. Our God did not leave us defenseless. If this is you, stop walking around with a spirit of defeat, and walk in the power that has been given unto you!

It never crossed Daniel's mind to do anything other than what he had always done.

Daniel 6:10 (NLT2)
¹⁰ But when Daniel learned that the law had been signed, he went home and knelt as usual in his upstairs room, with its windows open toward Jerusalem. He prayed three times a day, just as he had always done, giving thanks to his God. Daniel never wavered; the administrators and high officers' actions did not shake him. They stood together in agreement to sabotage Daniel while Daniel remained aligned with God. God had been faithful to Daniel; why risk depending on anything else other than God now?

King Belshazzar appointed Daniel as the third-highest ruler in the Kingdom; see Daniel 5:22 (NLT2). However, his position did not influence Daniel's service to God.

Godly Wisdom will always steer your actions. **Never allow position and status to change who you've been called to serve, how you serve,**

or the reason you serve. Living in an ungodly system (the world's) sometimes places God's children in situations where they must choose to stand for God's way or compromise with the world's ways and beliefs. Daniel's proof that we do not have to even at the threat of death. Are you bold and courageous enough not to compromise on what you know is right? The courage of wisdom will not allow you to consider an alternative plan that compromises your values. Wisdom is unwavering in its commitment to integrity, pushing you to stand firm even when the path ahead is challenging. Wisdom inspires a sense of courage and resolve that makes compromising one's values unthinkable.

Doing what's right will sometimes put you in a predicament, but know that if you do the righteous thing, God will not give you the victory. It may not always line up with your timing, but trust me, you win in the end. God has the power to cause you to prosper even in your place of hardship. If you are being treated unfairly keep doing your job and do it well. When people who mistreat you, keep being kind, continue to do the right thing. My husband and I have seen it happen in our own lives. Criticism, verbal attacks, lies, threats, but God always had our backs; God has always provided despite it all. When all was said and done, Daniel's enemies had been destroyed, thrown into the very den that was meant to take Daniel's life. Now, I'm not telling you God is going to kill your enemy; what I am telling you is that God will deal with them, and He will do it the way he deems fit. You do not need to concern yourself with that part; your job is to stay steadfast in your allegiance to all things God. It does not matter how God deals with them; the only thing that matters, is they cannot harm you when God has determined to protect you.

King Darius did just as King Nebuchadnezzar; bragged on Daniel's God acknowledging the power of His might, His never-ending rule, and His kingdom. That's the power of our God! The thing that has ruled over you has to acknowledge the power, authority, and reign of God and know they are no match for God! God will move in your life in such a powerful way that those who have no relationship or faith in God will have to acknowledge that He is God. Notice I said, "acknowledge He is God," because nowhere do we read that King Darius acknowledges God as His God; read it for yourself.

Daniel 6:26-27 (NLT2)
26 "I decree that everyone throughout my kingdom should tremble with fear before the God of Daniel. For he is the living God, and he will endure forever. His kingdom will never be destroyed, and his rule will never end.
27 He rescues and saves his people; he performs miraculous signs and wonders in the heavens and on earth. He has rescued Daniel from the power of the lions."

Your enemy may never accept God as their God, but they will have to acknowledge that He is God. That's on them, not you. Faith and courage matter, too; you cannot operate in wisdom without either, both will come under attack, and both will be tested. The one who walks in godly wisdom will know how to stand firm in the midst of the attacks. Please understand that warfare is fought on your knees in prayer, not with fleshly weaponry. You and I must continue to seek the face of God daily as Daniel and his friends did. We do not change our position or mindset in the midst of threats; instead, we stay the course and watch God do what He does best; turn a loss into a win. That's the wisdom of courage and faith.

One Last Thing: Our Definitive Example Of Walking In Wisdom.
Luke 2:41-52 (KJV)
41 Now his parents went to Jerusalem every year at the feast of the passover.
42 And when he was twelve years old, they went up to Jerusalem after the

custom of the feast.

⁴³ And when they had fulfilled the days, as they returned, the child Jesus tarried behind in Jerusalem; and Joseph and his mother knew not of it.

⁴⁴ But they, supposing him to have been in the company, went a day's journey; and they sought him among their kinsfolk and acquaintance.

⁴⁵ And when they found him not, they turned back again to Jerusalem, seeking him.

⁴⁶ And it came to pass, that after three days they found him in the temple, sitting in the midst of the doctors, both hearing them, and asking them questions.

⁴⁷ And all that heard him were astonished at his understanding and answers.

⁴⁸ And when they saw him, they were amazed: and his mother said unto him, Son, why hast thou thus dealt with us? behold, thy father and I have sought thee sorrowing.

⁴⁹ And he said unto them, How is it that ye sought me? wist ye not that I must be about my Father's business?

⁵⁰ And they understood not the saying which he spake unto them.

⁵¹ And he went down with them, and came to Nazareth, and was subject unto them: but his mother kept all these sayings in her heart.

⁵² And Jesus increased in wisdom and stature, and in favour with God and man.

Christ spiritual development began at an early age; even perplexing His parents by being positioned where He needed to be rather than where they thought He should be; as He astutely replied, "Wist not that I must be about my Father's business." We should all possess such wisdom to recognize our identity, purpose and responsibilities at such an early age.

Christ lived a life of obedience in constant alignment with God's will. Christ *only did what pleased His Father.* **John 8:29(KJV)**.

Remember even with the cross waiting on Him, alignment to God mattered. Jesus said," Nevertheless, Not My Will, But Thine Be Done" Luke 22:42 Wisdom will always necessitate God's will above your own, no matter how hard the assignment.

As believers, embracing God's wisdom will call for daily surrender and a willingness to follow His direction even when it challenges our personal desires or comfort. True spiritual growth stems not not merely from knowing the right thing to do but by consistently choosing to act upon it. Operating in wisdom may cost you comfort, but it will never result in regret, so choose wisely. There can never be a good enough excuse given that mandates yours or my disobedience. Divine guidance ensures our decisions align with His purpose and pleases God not what pleases us.

Closing Thoughts

It is my sincere hope that upon reading this book, you will engage in self-reflection to determine whether you have been relying more on your own wisdom rather than on God's wisdom. If you find the answer is a resounding yes, decide to let God take the lead and never again choose to be the navigator of your life and decisions. Allow Him to become the ultimate decision-maker for every choice you make. Every decision, regardless of the magnitude, warrants consideration and guidance from God. Sometimes, it is the decisions we consider insignificant that cause the most damage. Too often our decisions are driven by emotions. We get caught up in the 'I have to have it right now' syndrome instead of waiting for the right time to receive what we desire.

Receiving something at an inopportune time or season can become burdensome rather than become rather than a blessing. The ultimate pitfall would be to find yourself unprepared for a situation you believed you had adequately prepared for. This is why the wisdom of God is so important. We should never be so desperate to want anything outside the will and timing of God. No matter what we want in life, we must choose to like what God desires for us more. The end game is to be purposeful and successful in fulfilling God's plan for our lives. Adverse situations are the times when we are most desperate to find a resolution; they are also the times when we allow the weight of the moment to dictate our decision-making, which at times are driven by emotions rather than proper guidance.

In those moments, we need God's directives. God will reveal to you things about your circumstances you never considered. Only divine directive could have instructed Esther to host a banquet for her adversary, Haman, an act that led to his demise. I mean who wants to sit and dine with their enemy. (See Esther's full story in the book of Esther.) Only God would lead the children of Israel to the Red Sea to save their lives to take out their enemy. There are countless examples of God doing the unthinkable to rescue His children, resulting in extraordinary outcomes. God knows things we do not, so we must trust the wisdom that comes from God to lead us.

May the ideas outlined in this book serve as influential guiding principles that help you achieve success in areas where you have previously faced setbacks. May you be challenged to deepen your dependence upon God by accepting and applying the mandates, regulations, and established ways He has put in place to govern and better your life. The more space we allocate give to God to guide our lives, the less reliant we become human intellect. Yes, God does utilize others to fulfill His plans, however; its crucial to ensure that the individuals involved are His chosen vessels and not ones we have preselected. May you find joy and fulfillment as you move forward, having released complete control of your life into the hands of the person whose guidance is incomparable and unmatched.

ABOUT THE AUTHOR

Pamela R. Malone, affectionately known as Lady P, is the devoted wife of Apostle Carlos L. Malone Sr., Apostolic Overseer of The Bethel Church Miami. As an Elder in ministry, she faithfully serves alongside her husband, helping to advance the vision and mission of TBC with grace, wisdom, and compassion.

Lady P has a heart for empowering women and young girls to discover their God-given identity and purpose. She has served as Director of W.I.S.E. (Women in the Savior's Eyes) and is the founder of D.O.O.R. (Diamonds Out of the Rough), a ministry dedicated to supporting and guiding women as they pursue God and walk boldly in His calling for their lives.

Her passion for mentorship also inspired the creation of G.E.M.S. (Girls Equipped and Motivated to Succeed), a transformative program designed to nurture the spiritual, intellectual, and personal growth of young girls. In addition, Lady P has taught numerous leadership training sessions and New Discipleship classes, helping others strengthen their foundation in faith and leadership.

A dynamic and anointed teacher of the gospel, Lady P ministers with power, authenticity, and a unique voice that resonates deeply with those she reaches. Beyond the pulpit, she extends her ministry into the community by volunteering at The Agape Women Center, offering encouragement and hope to women overcoming mental health challenges and addiction. She believes deeply that in order to reach the world; one must be willing to go into the world.

Lady P credits her husband for inspiring and challenging her to walk fully in her purpose. Together, they share a beautiful family of five cherished children: Ashley, Andrea, Carlos Jr., Godson Raymond Young, and bonus son-in-love Derby Bernadel.

Her life's message can be summed up in one of her favorite quotes:

"God does not call the qualified; He qualifies the called."

www.ingramcontent.com/pod-product-compliance
Lightning Source LLC
Chambersburg PA
CBHW050914160426
43194CB00011B/2403